The Kitchen Table Classroom

How to Make Your HOME a SCHOOL

Dianne Wilton

Detselig Enterprises Ltd.

Calgary, Alberta, Canada

The Kitchen Table Classroom
© 2000 Dianne Wilton

Cataloguing Information in Publication
Wilton, Diane,
    The kitchen table classroom

Includes bibliographical references.
ISBN 1-55059-199-1
1. Home schooling. I. Title.
LC40.W54   2000   371.04'2   C00-910174-8

Detselig Enterprises Ltd.
210-1220 Kensington Rd. N.W.
Calgary, Alberta T2N 3P5
Telephone: (403) 283-0900
Fax: (403) 283-6947
E-mail: temeron@telusplanet. net
www.temerondetselig.com

We acknowledge the financial support of the Government of Canada through the Book Publishing Industry Development Program (BPIDP) for our publishing activities.

ISBN: 1-55059-199-1
SAN: 115-0324
Printed in Canada
Cover design by Dean Macdonald & Alvin Choong

Learning is a life-long activity...

Special thanks to my son, Dan, who "taught" me to how to write this book with encouragement, suggestions and patient editing

Dear Parents,

Why did I write this book? You've asked the teacher - maybe even me - to help your child out with his Math, her Reading, his Writing, her learning, but the best person to help your child out is you!

You may want to provide some help and practice with problem areas or want to give your child an edge with enrichment activities for those rainy Saturday afternoons. Or you may want some advice in using a structured home-school curriculum to let you teach at home, but still keep on track with the public system. Or you may want to join the ever-increasing number of totally home-schooled families, designing and taking responsibility for your own program. Whichever you choose, you have already made the most important choice... planning to take an active part in your child's education.

You have taught your children more than half of everything they will ever learn by the age of 5, and you definitely know your children better than anyone. You have their interests at heart, more than anyone else.

And you can do it!

I am going to fill you in on "how" children learn, "how" to put it into action, "how" to teach the basic subjects and "how" to integrate all subjects into a theme. But the most important "how" among them all will be

"how" to have fun with learning!

By bringing school into your home, you can do just that!

Sincerely,
Dianne Wilton

How . . .

Chapter 1

How to blend fun and learning...

Happiness
is a by-product which
sneaks up on you, unsought,
when you're busy at some-
thing else.

Betty Jane Wylie,
author

Chelsey is measuring
cinnamon for a double
batch of pumpkin muffins.

"Clang, clang, clang"—pot
lids and red banners
welcome the undulating
Chinese dragon.

Jillian and Jeffrey toss
balls into a net. Each
basket, 7 points, and they've
got 56 between them!

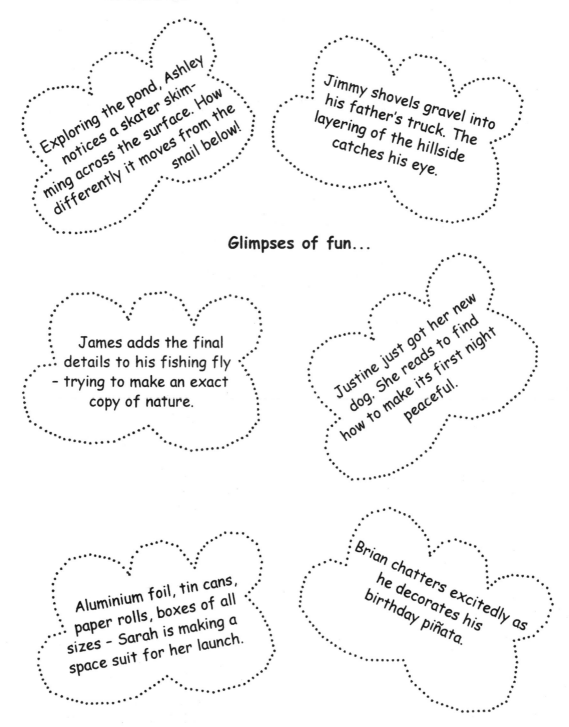

Exploring the pond, Ashley notices a skater skimming across the surface. How differently it moves from the snail below!

Jimmy shovels gravel into his father's truck. The layering of the hillside catches his eye.

Glimpses of fun...

James adds the final details to his fishing fly - trying to make an exact copy of nature.

Justine just got her new dog. She reads to find how to make its first night peaceful.

Aluminium foil, tin cans, paper rolls, boxes of all sizes - Sarah is making a space suit for her launch.

Brian chatters excitedly as he decorates his birthday piñata.

Jeremy carefully measures the strips for his box kite, concentrating on the directions in his library book.

Michael is designing a space station, using both his Lego and Meccano.

A rainbow has inspired Amanda to blend the colors in her paint box, with one color fading into the next.

Danny tries for a ball-bouncing world record. Can you hear him counting by 2's?

Peter is busy passing the tools while his Dad fixes his lawn mower.

Kevin is gathering eggs, grouping them into dozens. He hopes today's work will earn him enough money to buy that model tractor.

Marianna studies the individual snowflakes as they drift quietly onto her dark jacket.

. . . **Fun!**
But don't stop there . . .

Grasp these sparks of curiosity!

These are the opportunities to blend fun and learning. The children are already deeply involved, following their own interests. By sharing their excitement, we encourage them to expand these experiences even further.

Marianna might decide to use her geometric skills to design her own snowflakes. She might gather a bucket of snow to see how much water it would produce. She might measure the depth of snow in various areas of her yard or read to find why snow falls. She might draw graphs comparing the snowfall in different areas of the world. Listen to her, follow her ideas, help her locate information – your enthusiasm will be her motivation.

When your child is having fun, he is learning, following his curiosity. She is using Math while measuring, designing, graphing and comparing. He is writing to record his observations. She is reading to get more information. You can suggest other activities to integrate even more skills. If your child has been working with fractions, he might enjoy a snow-ball fight with you and his brother, each getting one-third of all the snowballs. If she is having difficulty writing complete sentences, she might want to list all that she has learned about snow, or write a letter telling her cousin in California about the snowfall. He could focus on the phonogram "ow" while writing a poem or dictating rhyming words on his tape recorder, or she could begin a collection of words beginning with "sn". Map work could be included as he learns about snow in other areas of the world.

Activities of "fun " are opportunities for learning. By integrating the basic skills with your child's interests, learning is kept alive and fun. You are helping to create life-long learners.

Chapter 2

How to set your table...

Before everything else, getting ready is the secret of success.

Henry Ford

First, decide the extent to which you want to be involved in your child's education – which "set of dishes" you want to use:

☞ **Do you want to design your own home-schooling program?** Great! Whether you are just beginning this adventure into learning, or whether you are looking for new ideas to enliven your present school at home, this book will provide many practical suggestions.

Watch to see what your child is interested in. Listen to him talk. See what fascinates him. Ask him what he wants to know more about. Get these ideas down – yes, they will evolve and change, but make a list. The ideas will be exciting and will be the base for your program.

Now, read over the teaching suggestions for mathematics, reading, and writing. Be aware of the required skills so that you can integrate them into your child's activities in a logical sequence.

Most importantly, watch to see how your child learns. Does he work best visually, physically, from an artistic angle . . . does she learn by analyzing and synthesizing . . . does he need to manipulate concrete objects for long periods of time? Be alert to his pace and his learning style. Design your program around your child's strengths, following her from success to success.

☞ **Do you and your child want to work at home, but feel more comfortable using prescribed materials to keep you on track?** If you're feeling unsure of what to teach, this is a good way to begin home schooling. There are many independent course materials to choose from, such as "Saxon Math," "Math-U-See" or "Hooked on Phonics." Talking to other home schoolers and looking through commercial packages will help you decide which programs will work best for your child. Some sources are included in this book - write to them for specific information (and samples, if possible), but don't get buried under a mountain of programs. Start with one and supplement it with ideas from this book. An important warning here is to not let your child's learning become too compartmentalized, keeping each subject separate from the other. Integrate materials into a theme or project, putting your child's interests and needs at the center of your program.

Many of the provinces in Canada have distance education programs available which can often be adapted to suit the individual family. These complete programs are based on the educational requirements for each province. By following them, you can be certain to stay in your public school stream. You may choose to use an Internet-based school to provide structure.

Be sure, however, to always stay on the track of your child. It is not enough to teach subjects. You can use prescribed programs successfully by supplementing them with meaningful activities to support your child's strengths and styles of learning. Your child must play a vital role in his home-based education!

☞ **Is your goal to help your school-attending child master those basic skills?** Good for you! Catch problems early, keeping his learning experiences positive. Set up an appointment for you and your child to meet with the classroom teacher. The three of you have a mutual goal!

As a group, list the difficulties your child is having. Arrange these in order of difficulty so that your child can check them off as he masters each one. Find out how the teacher is dealing with these concerns. Then, by starting where your child is successful, and watching to see how she learns best, you can supplement the schoolwork with purposeful strategies at home. Use this book to help you get organized, following the specific subject areas and the learning activities which will most help your child.

If motivation is a problem, make the learning meaningful by incorporating the school exercises into a theme of his choice.

☞ **Do you want to provide that "extra edge" to revitalize your child's learning?** Your child may be doing wonderfully well with his schoolwork, but you can enrich those experiences even further.

Follow up the classroom topics with extra projects, relating specifically to her interests. For example, if she is studying Ancient Greece in school, help her find a book at the library on Greek myths. He may enjoy the geometric look of Grecian art, using a similar style to design his own urn. She may want to compare ancient Greek society to her own lifestyle. Or he might want to learn more about Greece today. Visit a travel agent together for brochures or posters. Encourage her to write to the Greek consulate. Go out for a Greek meal, or follow a recipe to make moussaka. Learn some games and a few words in Greek. Or an entirely new interest may spark. Follow it and enjoy! The possibilities are endless. Learning becomes relevant, meaningful and fun.

> If a child is to keep alive his inborn sense of wonder without any such gift from the fairies, he needs the companionship of at least one adult who can share it, rediscovering with him the joy, excitement and mystery of the world we live in.
>
> Rachel Carson

The next important step in "setting your table" is to organize your time to fit this important commitment into your busy life. By planning ahead and by integrating your child's education into family and business activities, you can accomplish a lot.

- **Saturday adventures?** Know what you're doing, where you're going, what you'll need and where you'll get what you need. If you have other chores which must be done that day, try to include them in the total learning adventure. Make the whole time count.

- **Working on specific skills after school?** Plan each lesson with a clear procedure in mind. Have all your materials ready so that your child can make good use of this valuable time. Make your sessions short and focused. Schedule a certain time each day, a time which is good for both you and your child. Let your friends know when you'll be working, asking them to call at other times. Use an answering machine, with its volume turned low to keep the telephone distraction down. If you have other children, ask them to not interrupt, and if necessary, assign activities for them to pursue independently at this time. Provide toddlers with a special basket of their own "work." You can include crayons, paper, some attractive blocks, old magazines, a favorite book, home-made play dough, whatever your child will play with quietly and safely. Be sure to give them plenty of attention later, showing your appreciation.

- **Totally home-schooling?** Your daily schedule will largely depend on your family life-style and particular circumstances, but try to be consistent with specific times each day for planning and for concentrated study. Model the art of list-making and help your child make his own list of things to do each day, checking them off as they are completed and transferring left-overs to the next day. This planning time is best at the start or end of each day. As well, consider weekly, monthly and yearly schedules. You may want to work four days of the week, reserving the fifth day for special events. Some families "work" a six-day week, and take a whole week off each month. Or you may want to schedule short holiday breaks throughout the year. Have your child help to plan his "school" year, laying it out on the calendar. One of the advantages to home-schooling is this flexibility of scheduling.

- **Home schooling more than one child?** You can half your preparation time by using a theme-approach. This may be difficult if each child has different interests, but try alternating themes or broadening them to include a variety of topics. For example, if your daughter wants to learn more about the ocean and your son is curious about space, you could either study the ocean one month and the next, space. Or they might compromise with a theme of stars, learning about stars in the sky, starfish, movie stars, star patterns in nature, etc. Whichever way it works for your family, it will help to organize activities if there is a common theme. Each of your children will participate in the theme at different levels, according to their skills and interests within that subject.

- **Schedule quiet periods into your child's day.** Too often children are short-changed by being in so many clubs and activities that they don't have time to reflect and to investigate on their own. Give your child space and time to think about his experiences. Let her assimilate all that she has learned – this is where connections are made, and with those, personal satisfaction.

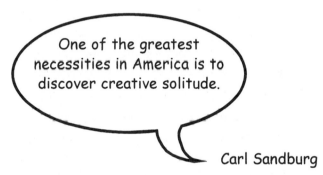

One of the greatest necessities in America is to discover creative solitude.

Carl Sandburg

As well as organizing your time, you will want to set up your space and supplies to make your program efficient and effective. Just as you need ingredients to bake a cake, or tools to build a fence, you also need equipment to "make" a home into a school. Fortunately, you already have most of what you need! All you have to do is organize your environment so that it is safe and stimulating.

- **A quiet space,** free from distractions, should be designated as the place for short lessons and focused practice sessions. It could be a certain chair at your kitchen table, a bedroom desk, or a corner in the living room. If you're sailing, it could be the floor of the cabin. If you're on a tropical island, choose a spot under a specific palm tree. It doesn't matter where it is, but be sure it's comfortable, well-lit and a pleasant place to be. Try to stick to that same place each day, so that it becomes associated with concentration.

- **A large box or basket** can keep your tools together. Let the type of these supplies reflect the ages of the student – a younger child's paste should be substituted for a glue stick for an older child; thick felt pens for a younger child, but thin felt pens for the older.

Arrange your tools so that you don't waste valuable time searching for the eraser or paper clips. Have all sharpened pencils and pens together in a bottle. Use a zip-lock bag for small items such as paper clips, glue sticks, eraser, pencil sharpener, etc. Place all papers and exercise books together. Let the ruler stand up along the edge of the box so that it can be easily grasped.

Encourage your child to take responsibility for replacing all materials where they belong at the end of each session. At first, you will have to show this by example, doing it in a matter of fact but pleasant manner. The next time, replace the materials in partnership with your child, relaxing as you both put the supplies away. Sit with him as he does it the next time, giving him praise and encouragement. Soon, he will be doing it on his own. Tell your child why the supplies are organized so precisely. When he sits down each day, he will be able to immediately start work.

☞ **Books are valuable resources**. Gradually collect as many new and attractive books as you can, but also keep your eye on garage sales, library-discard sales, and second-hand book stores. Gather books below your child's reading level (for those lazy, hazy days), books at the level she most often reads, and books above his level (to challenge and to read together). Collect books for yourself and for the rest of the family to enjoy. This permanent collection will encourage everyone to read old favorites time and time again.

Magazine and newspaper subscriptions are great year-round gifts, for both you and your children. Let your family and friends know of your child's interests, whether it's in sports, arts and crafts, or nature. Some families find that sharing news items is a great way to stimulate conversation at the supper table. Everyone takes turns telling what they've learned in the newspaper or magazine that day.

Keep a globe and world atlas handy. They will help your child to relate information to locations in the world. Include good quality dictionaries, at both adult and child levels.

As well, be sure to borrow books from the public library. You can often take out excessive amounts of books, exposing new ideas and interests.

Over time, browsing through a lot of books will help him to recognize books of quality. For those occasional projects, such as making a kite, cooking a Japanese dish or designing an Indian mask, the public library will be an invaluable source of information.

Be sure your reading material is easily accessible in a well-used room of your "school" and organized in a meaningful way. Put the "how to" books together, both adults' and children's. Have a special basket or shelf for magazines. Designate a specific spot on your bookshelves for the globe, atlas, and dictionaries. Keep your library books on a separate shelf. Your child should be able to easily find what he needs, yet not face a daunting chore when replacing them.

- **Puzzles, cards and games** provide hours of fun learning opportunities. As you develop themes, you and your family will enjoy adding to this collection with home-made versions.

  Jigsaw puzzles will have a longer life if the backs of each puzzle piece are marked to identify the puzzle to which it belongs. You can use color or symbol coding. The individual puzzles can then be stored in zip-lock bags with the corresponding code glued to the bag.

- **Collections** can be organized into labeled shoeboxes or displayed on labeled shelves. Your family may have a coin or stamp collection. Your child could collect rocks, leaves, shells, or abandoned bird nests. The important thing is to keep "like" materials together, so that they have value as a collection.

- **Building and designing toys**, such as Lego and Meccano, give your child many opportunities for developing creativity and imagination. Science, Math, Art and Social Studies are all happening as he plays. The manipulation of the small pieces helps to refine his skills in fine-motor control, as well. Never underestimate the value of well-designed toys! See-through containers will keep these in good condition and attractively stored.

- **Household tools and supplies** play an important role in making learning "real." Be sure that the tools and appliances which are available for the child to use are in good repair and are neatly organized. Sort nuts and bolts, screws, nails, pasta, beans, buttons, elastic bands, toothpicks and wire ties into labeled jars or margarine containers. With this organization already in place, your child will form the habit of handling and replacing materials carefully.

☞ **Items of technology** are great motivators. A basic tape recorder encourages reading and listening activities and spelling and math drills, and helps to develop good speaking skills.

An easy-to-use camera will refine your child's observation skills, encouraging her to notice the intricate details of a flower, record building construction over time, report on experiments, etc. Taking photographs provides the motivation to complete a hike to the top of the mountain or to write a letter showing Grandma his newly-designed spacecraft. "Creative Memory Albums" are opportunities to combine organizational and artistic talents.

A computer adds another dimension of learning. Basic programming, word-processing, access to the Internet, and educational games are all incentives. If you don't have a computer of your own, check with the library or recreational center in your area. They will provide assistance and they often make computers available free of charge.

☞ **Large-motor equipment and space for physical activity** will round out your child's development. Be sure an open area is available for running and skipping. A local park or gym with climbing apparatus is a plus. Provide your child with time to pursue a sport of his own interest - skiing, swimming, soccer, badminton, dance, etc. Besides building strength and confidence and having fun, your child will be learning at the same time. Concepts of physics and biology are absorbed incidentally from an interaction with large-motor equipment. Often, other skills can be incorporated, such as skip-counting or rhyming while hopping, running and skipping. Many children learn best when they are physically active and much research has shown that an active body develops an active mind.

Now your table is set. You know which set of dishes to use and how to organize the items making up your set. You are ready for success!

Chapter 3

How to add the ingredients for success . . .

It's fun when you're winning.

Jacques Plant,
hockey player

1. **Enthusiasm is by far the most important ingredient in your "school."** Become involved with the interests of your child. Listen to him, and let his enthusiasm become yours!

- **Support her ideas.** Recognize and support different ways of doing tasks, encouraging your child's initiative and creativity. Follow her suggestions. There's never just one way to learn or to do an activity.

- **Recognize his efforts with praise and appreciation.** Use deserved praise, finding specific aspects which you honestly like – the effective use of red and green next to each other in his art pattern, the attractive layout of his relief map, the care he showed in writing all the numerals neatly and correctly, the thinking he showed by arranging the leaves the way he did. Put these words of appreciation into written messages, either directly on his work or on Post-it Notes.

- **Display her work** in a visible spot so that it can be acknowledged by other members of the family. (Better still, encourage him to set up the display.)

- **Value his accomplishments.** Using file folders, collect a selection of your child's dated work periodically, in both writing and math. Have him take part in choosing which samples should be included in this record-keeping. He will likely want to store some of his posters and art work as well, possibly rolled up in map tubes.

☞ **Celebrate the "extras"** of her enriched experiences. Culminate a theme or unit of work with a splash, incorporating all that she has enjoyed. It might be the construction of a mural for the wall, a family dinner, or a party with her friends. This is a time for assimilation, and will allow her to reflect upon all she has learned.

☞ **Emphasize personal satisfaction**. If your child feels good about what he has done, he will have a sense of personal fulfillment (just as you feel if you've made a beautiful layer cake, got your photos all labeled and organized, got the grass looking perfect) – This is real motivation! Encourage him to stay tuned to his feelings.

☞ **Stars, stickers and stamps** can be used to recognize your child's efforts, but don't rely on these completely. If he is having fun, and is feeling good about his work, your enthusiasm will be a more sustaining motivation.

☞ **Earned days off and special activities** can be used to revitalize slacking motivation. "When you finish this, we can . . ." often helps you to move forward.

☞ **Recognize his strengths and give positive feedback** as soon as possible. Watch him as he begins his task and give constructive comments immediately. Don't let him waste time practicing something incorrectly. As soon as he feels confident, encourage him to finish the task independently, and to mark his own work. Advise him to use a red dot rather than an X, changing it easily into a ✓ when corrected. A circle around a misspelled word or error in grammar can become a happy face when corrected ☺. It is important for you to give prompt feedback on his finished task, but let that feedback be positive, geared towards what he has accomplished. Be sure that he sees himself as a successful learner.

2. **Follow your child's pace.**

☞ **Begin at his success level!** Start with what your child does well, giving him many experiences at that level to build his confidence. We do what we like to do, and we only like to do what we can be successful at. So in order for your child to do his best learning, he must like learning. In order for him to like learning, he must be successful at learning!

- **Gradually add new skills**, letting her meet with success at each step. If she begins to make errors, the work is either too difficult at this time, or there is just too much of it. Return to a previous step for more practice, or break the assignment into smaller units. Always work at her success level.

- **Don't let outside expectations get in the way**. Even if Aunt Mary insists that Joanne should be able to read by now, be firm in your position that Joanne will show you when she is able to read. This does not mean that you should simply sit back and wait. By moving at her pace, through a series of steps, with pauses for practice, you will be helping her to be successful all along the way. Her confidence will be maintained, and she will want to practice because she is having fun. She is having fun because she is meeting success!

- **Learning happens in spurts**. Leap onto the spurt and go with it. Then relax, and let it seep in. The mind needs time to assimilate and associate new things learned. Give your child space, time and respect.

- **Trust that your child will be successful**. Children instinctively reflect your attitudes. You, as your child's teacher, must accept that we all learn at different rates and at different times. If you are feeling impatient or worrying about the progress of your child, he, too, will feel that there's something to worry about. A child must feel secure with his abilities, and not be made to feel as if he's slow or lazy. Work at your child's pace, relax and enjoy his learning. A Chinese proverb reminds us *"With time and patience, the mulberry leaf becomes a silk gown."*

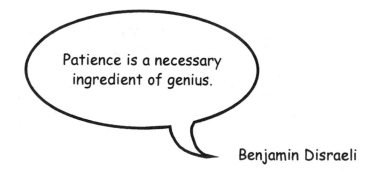

Patience is a necessary ingredient of genius.

Benjamin Disraeli

3. Follow your child's style of learning.

☞ **Your child is unique**. You have discovered this time and time again. What worked for one child, didn't work for her. What sparked him, didn't interest another. A cactus thrives in sandy soil and dry conditions, while a fern only fully develops in rich soil and rain; so, too, one child will thrive given hands-on activities while another will learn best by making up rhymes and songs. There is no "best" way to learn for everyone . . . Katie learns most easily by moving her muscles, skipping rope as she counts by fives. Jeffrey's strength is in art, learning the times tables as he finds patterns in the multiplication chart. Look at the tree chart (facing page) to see the different ways in which your child might learn the names of the trees.

Throughout the subject chapters, I will give plenty of examples which pertain to different learning styles. Use the strategies which bring him success most easily, but include projects for all areas of development – physical, mental, emotional and social.

4. Make her learning activities meaningful.

☞ **Involve him in your family business**, or encourage him to set up his own business, baking pies for sale, shoveling snow, walking dogs, selling craft items, etc.

☞ **Give her a reason to count money**, suggesting that she can pay for the groceries once she has learned to count it out, or she can buy a certain item when she has saved enough money for it.

☞ **Give him a reason to read**, finding a book on kite construction, following a recipe for her favorite cookies, or leaving messages for him on the refrigerator, such as "There's some cake on the counter – you can have a piece yourself and give a piece to your friend."

☞ **Give her a reason to write**, suggesting that she write for information about tulips when she decides to plant a bulb garden, or a letter to the Chinese Consulate to get New Year celebration details for her theme development. Encourage her to write to her grandparents or cousins or pen pals to invite them for a visit. Ask her to write out the grocery list for you, or a favorite recipe to give to a friend.

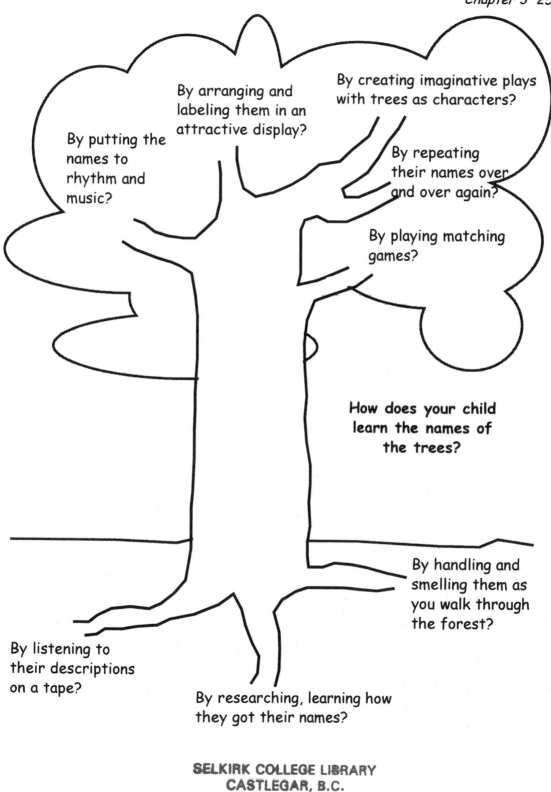

- **Capitalize on her interests**. Does she like skipping? Make some chants for skip-counting. (2, 4, 6, 8 Who do we appreciate?) Help her to create her own chants on tape or encourage her to teach her friends.

- **Move from the concrete to the abstract**. While presenting new concepts to your child, always begin with the concrete, something he can directly relate to. This will help him to understand later abstract representations. Don't hurry through the manipulation of objects when learning Math ideas. Help him to set up the decimal system using toothpicks and elastic bands, preparing him for the processes of "borrowing" and "carrying." Let him use buttons, apples, candies, stickers, etc. to work with fractions and arithmetic operations. Encourage him to work through his understanding of word problems by acting the problem out, later drawing pictures of the action and finally, writing the action in symbolic form. In learning about the world, help her to draw the continents and oceans on a grapefruit, then flatten the peel to see the world as a flat map. Have fun making a solar system model, using papier-maché. By moving from three-dimensional representations to two-dimensional pictures and charts, and finally to abstract ideas, learning will be meaningful.

5. **Ensure that he has lots of opportunities for practice.**

- A gymnast or pianist puts in hours and hours of practice and concentration. Repetition puts their motions into memory. Practice is necessary for learning, too. It puts the facts, the skills and the processes into memory.

- Provide lots of practice in answering what, when, where, how and why questions, both verbal and written. People often find application forms or exam writing difficult simply because they haven't learned to look at and answer exactly what is being asked.

- Practice the facts in a variety of ways, making repetition fun.

6. **Encourage her independence.**

- Encourage your child to play an active role in all aspects of his program, setting the schedule, displaying his accomplishments, developing themes and collecting materials.

- Give very clear directions when you assign tasks, having her repeat your instructions before she begins. Then, encourage her to work as independently as possible, with few interruptions.

- Provide ways for him to mark his own work, through self-correcting games and activities (if it's wrong, the puzzle just won't fit together; the answers on the back of the pie plates don't match his), or through specific answer sheets. He may enjoy using calculators and tape recordings to correct his own work.

- Give him skills to evaluate his own writing abilities. These will be detailed in the chapter "How to weave thinking into writing . . ."

- Help her to take on increasing responsibilities within the family and community. This develops independence and self-confidence, important prerequisites in learning.

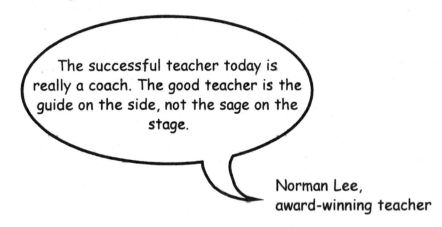

The successful teacher today is really a coach. The good teacher is the guide on the side, not the sage on the stage.

Norman Lee,
award-winning teacher

7. Chart your journey.

- It is important for your child to recognize his accomplishments. He might like to list his activities each day on a rolled banner, highlighting important successes over the week. She might prefer to design her storage box with a series of stepping stones, stamped to recognize each day or each activity. Encourage him to create his own fun way to visually acknowledge his progress and successes.

- You, too, will be better able to support your child's learning if you have a visual representation of how much learning occurs each day. Set up a log book and each day, fill in both formal and incidental activities for each subject.

October 5 to October 11						
Math	Reading	Writing	Social Studies	Science	Art	Physical Education
Counted seeds by 2s	Read to my sister	Shopping list	Drama of first Thanks- giving	Egg ex- periments	Feather painting	Soccer
Doubled recipe	Went to library	"oo" poem	Map of community	Planted seeds	Seed mosaic	Monkey bars

Once you are confident with your home schooling, and recognize just how much is being accomplished, you can move to a more simplified form of record keeping.

	Math	Reading	Writing	Social Studies	Science	Art	Physical Educ.
October 5	√ √ √	√ √ √ √ √	√ √	√ √	√ √ √ √ √	√	√ √ √
October 6	√ √	√ √ √	√ √ √	√	√ √	√ √	√ √ √ √

Occasionally, you may want to check on the completeness of your program, isolating specific areas of development. A circle wheel is described in "to sim-mer it all together" to help with your assessment.

8. Pursue your own dreams.

☞ In order to be a happy teacher, you must be a happy person. Set aside two hours a week just for you. Cut down on your "have to" list, prioritiz-ing things which should get done. Schedule your own time for exercise and relaxation.

☞ Take up an interest which you've always wanted to follow. While you are working towards your own accomplishments, you are providing your child with a model for enjoyable learning and achievement.

**By providing the ways for your child to be successful,
you have made learning fun!
When learning is fun, the cycle is set . . .**

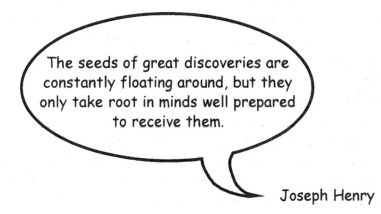

Chapter 4

How to measure in Mathematics . . .

The seeds of great discoveries are constantly floating around, but they only take root in minds well prepared to receive them.

Joseph Henry

Math is a part of life . . .

Your child began learning math concepts even before he knew about numbers – he sorted his cars, shared his cookies, and compared the size of his dog and cat. Later, she counted pennies and measured how tall she was on her growth chart. He added the red jelly beans to the yellow, and subtracted as he ate them. She counted by 2s while skipping rope. He became aware of fractions as he looked over the equal pieces of pizza. Waiting for her friend to come over, she learned about time. These incidental activities are the base of formal operations: This is Math. In order for this natural learning to develop further, continue to let Math be a part of life, encouraging your child to explore his own strategies to solve problems. Everyday activities (comparing prices to get the most from an allowance or the best buy for a pair of skis, tallying statistics while sorting baseball cards, multiplying to group snowballs, dividing out marbles) provide the best opportunities to embed Math into meaningful content. Set up a bird feeder and have your child count and classify the birds, comparing the number of blue jays and chickadees, noticing how many birds arrive one day compared to another, calculating how much seed is eaten on an average day and how many days a bag of seed should last, determining how much it costs to feed the birds per day. We can help him use symbols and equations to represent what he learns, writing the numbers and + sign when he puts his red and blue cars into one box, the x sign as she doubles the cake recipe, and the ÷ sign as he distributes his cookies.

A family business, or your child's business or hobby, provides real experiences with Math. Some children are able to sell eggs or produce from their gardens. Others have used their cooking, carpentry and knitting skills to sell items at craft sales. Others are into yard work or dog-walking. In pricing their goods and services, they become aware of value, recognizing that multi-packs are usually the best buy, but not always! They learn to balance their check books and keep an account of expenses and credits.

Learning efficient methods of calculation will help your child meet the immediate needs of his everyday life. When Steven wanted to know how many stamps he could place in his stamp booklet, he wasn't looking forward to counting 24 eight times. He was glad to learn a short cut, multiplication. Janie was ready to learn a new addition calculation when she wanted a total price for her computer supplies. Brian needed to know how to calculate area for his neighborhood grass-cutting business. When Maria wanted to distribute an equal amount of candy in her birthday bags, she was anxious to learn a quick way to divide 135 by 9. Jamie was glad to learn about equivalent fractions when the pizza arrived. Use these genuine learning opportunities!

Math is cumulative . . .

Although some steps in Math often lead to others, there is no absolute order in which individual concepts need to be taught. Certain skills, however, do depend on previous Math experiences. For this reason, I have included a sequence chart, not to use rigidly, but as a guide. When your child wants to subtract two numbers which require regrouping, it is important that she is confident with the simple concept of taking things away, and has already had many experiences with place value. If he needs to calculate the area of a lawn, he should already know how to multiply. He will then only require activities discovering that area is equal to the length times the width. The sequence chart will help determine prerequisite skills. Teaching Math concepts as they come up in daily experiences is more effective than by following a rigid hierarchy, but

	Adding/Subtracting	Multiplying/Dividing	Fractions	Integers

Problem-Solving
 	
Graphing
 	
Measuring
  length
  money
  time
  temperature
  perimeter
  area
  volume
 	
Estimating
	Counting objects, relating the amount to its numeral
	
	Counting objects in sets, relating total amount
	
	Adding and Subtracting 1-digit numbers (5 + 7), (8 – 3)
	
	Place Value
	Adding and Subtracting multi-digit numbers without regrouping (36 + 22), (36 – 22)
	
	Adding multi-digit numbers with regrouping (354 + 107)
	
	Subtracting multi-digit numbers with regrouping (36-29)
	
	Subtracting multi-digit numbers with 0 in the top number (50–26), (506-238)
	
	Adding decimals
	
	Subtracting decimals
		Counting objects in equal sets
		
		Multiplying and dividing number facts (3 × 7), (21 ÷ 7)
		
		Place Value – breaking numbers into units, tens, hundreds, etc.
		
		Multiplying by a 1-digit number without regrouping (83 × 2)
		
		Multiplying by a 1-digit number with regrouping (83 × 6)
		
		Multiplying by multi-digit numbers without regrouping (32 × 12)
		
		Multiplying by multi-digit numbers with regrouping (38 × 25)
		
		Dividing by a 1-digit divisor (636 ÷ 4)
		
		Dividing by multi-digit divisors (234 ÷ 15)
		
		Multiplying and dividing with decimals (5.9 × 4.3)
			Dividing an object into equal parts $\frac{1}{4}$
			
			Dividing a number of objects into equal parts 3/5
			
			Equivalent fractions (1/2 = 5/10)
			
			Adding and Subtracting fractions
			- with same denominator (1/6 + 3/6)
			- with different denominators (3/4 – $\frac{1}{2}$)
			-with mixed numbers (2 1/5 + 7 9/10)
			
			Multiplying fractions (2/6 × $\frac{1}{4}$)
			
			Dividing fractions (5/8 ÷ 1/3)
			
			Multiplying and dividing mixed numbers (6 2/3 × 5 1/6)
				Number line showing positive and negative integers from zero
				
				Adding positive integers (6 + 8)
				
				Adding negative integers (-6 + -8)
				
				Adding positive and negative integers (6 + -8)
				
				Subtracting positive integers (5 – 2)
				
				Subtracting negative integers (-5 - -2)
				
				Subtracting positive and negative integers (8 - -3)
				
				Multiplying and dividing positive integers (6 × 2), (6 ÷ 2)
				
				Multiplying and dividing negative integers (-6 × -2)
				
				Multiplying and dividing positive and negative integers (9 ÷ -3)

check where your child is within the general sequence. Your lessons should be short. If a skill comes up which requires a lot of time and previous learning, he will wonder if the calculation is worth it after all. For now, simply give your child the answer or let him work it out manually. Plan to return to the needed skills at another time.

Keep this sequence chart handy. You can then integrate appropriate math lessons into her daily activities or themes. While baking cookies, she might learn addition, or she might subtract, divide, multiply, or even use fractions and decimals. While experimenting with kites, linear measurement and geometry will likely be high on the list, but you can also include arithmetic operations as he works with the tail ribbons, alters sizes, or compares flight times. Start with what your child already knows, and add the next step. This will ensure many of the basics are covered before more complex ideas are encountered.

Some Math skills do need to be taught . . .

Although this book is not a manual of rules, it is important for your child to have a solid understanding of basic Math concepts. A "cookbook" with "recipes" to teach each lesson may seem desirable at first, but with this, you are forgetting the most important factor: your child. The following methods will guide you in teaching the arithmetic calculations, but use these suggestions with your child's style and pace in mind.

Make your lessons focused, and start with what he already knows. Watch her as she solves everyday Math problems. Better than any test, ask your child to describe each step he takes as he performs an operation. You will be able to see exactly how she is thinking, and be able to recognize misconceptions and to detour around difficulties. When he completely understands one skill, you can then add the next step.

You may have to look at one lesson in isolation at first, but always be sure to follow up by integrating it into his everyday activities or themes. In order to learn Math, children have to experience it in their everyday lives. Provide lots of time for your child to manipulate, to explore and to practice. It's a process of construction.

1. Teaching Place Value:

When children begin to count objects, they relate quantities to numerals. It is difficult, however, to visualize just how many objects "4238" is. Your child needs many experiences with concrete objects, grouping by 10s, 100s and 1000s to understand what large numerals actually represent. Fortunately, you have the perfect objects to work with, right in your kitchen – toothpicks and elastic bands:

a. Have your child count toothpicks until she gets 10. Then wrap an elastic band around them to make a bundle of ten. As she continues to count single toothpicks, she will have 1 bundle of ten and 1 single (11), 1 ten and 2 (12), 1 ten and 3 (13). Develop the teens in this way, writing the symbol for each number as it is formed with toothpicks.

10	11	12	13	14...

b. Continue counting toothpicks up to 20. Wrap a second elastic band around the ten single toothpicks, and you now have two bundles of ten. Keep counting to show 2 groups of ten and 1 (21), 2 tens and 2 (22), 2 tens and 3 (23) . . . 8 tens and 2 (82) . . .

20	21	22	23	24...

c. When 10 groups of 10 are formed, she will have reached the "magic" ten again, and can put a large elastic band around the 10 bundles. Counting them all, either individually or by 10s, she'll know she has 1 large bundle of 100 individual toothpicks.

10 tens   =   100

By following this detailed procedure, your child is acquiring concrete knowledge of what numerals mean. Engage the whole family in counting and grouping through the hundreds, and possibly, thousands (lots of toothpicks!). Don't try to do it all in one day. Let it grow and become a part of an experience over days. Although this may sound tedious, make it a game; it is an important basis for future learning. By recognizing that "4238" is 4 thousands, 2 hundreds, 3 tens and 8 ones, the calculations for addition, subtraction, multiplication and division will make sense. It is an important prerequisite for these large number operations.

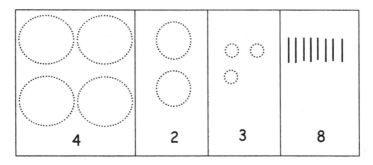

2. Teaching Addition:

Children learn the concept of adding when they put one group of things with another group, and then count out the total amount. When they want to add 62 objects and 23 objects, however, they would need to do a lot of counting to get the sum. Now, they are ready to learn the "quick way" to add, the addition algorithm:

a. First, choose two numbers which will add together without having to form any new bundles of toothpicks (none of the digits add up to more than 9), such as 62 + 23. Help your child make "62" using 6 bundles of 10 toothpicks and 2 single toothpicks. Then make "23" the same way. Now he can count all the single toothpicks together first, and then all of the bundles of 10 together. Show this in symbolic form, right beside the toothpicks.

62	6 tens 2 ones	62
+ 23	+ 2 tens 3 ones	23
	8 tens 5 ones	85

Give your child lots of time for practice with numerals which do not require regrouping toothpicks into new bundles of tens. Try (327 + 251), (4561 + 4237), and (12345 + 54321).

```
      327        =      3 hundreds 2 tens 7 ones        327
+     251        =      2 hundreds 5 tens 1 one         251
                       5 hundreds 7 tens 8 ones         578
```

b. By now, your child will want to solve her own addition questions, but these will often require regrouping. She wants to move ahead! Once again, build the numerals with the toothpicks and add. Emphasize that the single toothpicks must be added first. This time, whenever the sum reaches a "ten," she can make a new bundle and put it with the other "tens." Write the operation with symbols, as well.

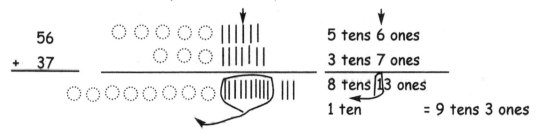

```
   56                              5 tens 6 ones
+  37                              3 tens 7 ones
                                   8 tens 13 ones
                          1 ten        = 9 tens 3 ones
```

c. Finally, discuss the "quick way" to add. Show that the symbol representing the new bundle of ten can be placed above the column of the other "tens" and added as another "ten." You may know this as "carrying." She has now just learned it by regrouping, and understands how it works.

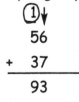

```
     ①
     56
+    37
     93
```

3. Teaching Subtraction:

Subtraction is the opposite of addition, starting with a large quantity and taking away a smaller amount. Again, children learn the concept at an early age through daily experiences. To learn the calculation, begin with concrete materials and develop the symbolic representation alongside, as you did with addition.

a. Pose a question which does not need regrouping (the top digit is larger than the lower digit in each column), such as 72-41. Make the numeral "72" with bundles of toothpicks, and then take 41 of those toothpicks away, starting with the ones.

```
  72                                              72
-  41                                           -  41
 ----                                            ----
                                                  31
```

b. Other questions will require regrouping. When your child needs to take more single toothpicks away than there are (the lower digit is greater than the upper digit) such as in 65 - 29, discuss how he could get more single toothpicks. He will likely suggest that he unwrap one of the bundles of ten.

```
  65                                              65
-  29                                           -  29
 ----                                            ----
                                                  36
```

1. we don't have enough ones
2. get some more ones   *(15 total)*
3. subtract 9 ones now   *(15 - 9 = 6)*
4. subtract 2 tens now   *(5 - 2 = 3)*

c. After your child has practiced this regrouping subtraction, pose a question with a zero in the larger number (302 - 165). Encourage her to find a solution to this new complication. Guide her towards simply ungrouping the next column, or even the next one, to get enough toothpicks to be able to subtract.

```
  2  → 10              9 →12
  3 H  0 T  2    =    2 H  10 T  2    =    2 H  9 T  12
- 1 H  6 T  5    =    1 H   6 T  5    =    1 H  6 T   5
 ------------         -------------        -------------
                                           1 H  3 T   7
```

d. Show the algorithm with symbols only, and she will now be able to tackle any subtraction problem.

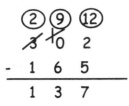

$$
\begin{array}{ccc}
② & ⑨ & ⑫ \\
\not{3} & \not{1}0 & 2 \\
- \ 1 & 6 & 5 \\
\hline
1 & 3 & 7
\end{array}
$$

4. Teaching Multiplication:

When your child places 5 chocolate chips on each of 4 cupcakes and knows it will take 20 chips, he is multiplying. He might count individually, or begin to skip-count (5, 10, 15, 20). Either way, he is learning what multiplication means.

When he wants to know how many chocolate chips will be needed to have 12 chips on each of the 4 cupcakes, he will be happy to learn a more efficient solution than counting. Now is the time to teach the multiplication algorithm. If your child has had few "toothpick" experiences, review place value to be sure he has a good understanding of our number system. If he has been building numbers with toothpicks and manipulating these toothpicks as he adds and subtracts, the multiplication algorithm will be a logical step.

a. To calculate 4 x 12, make 4 sets of 12 toothpicks, using tens and ones. Total the ones (8 ones) and total the tens (4 tens), and pull them together into one set of 48. Now write it in words, showing how the child first totaled the four sets of ones, then the four sets of tens. This is multiplication.

$$
\begin{array}{r}
12 \\
\times \ \ 4 \\
\hline
\end{array}
$$

$$
\begin{array}{r}
1 \text{ ten } \ 2 \text{ ones} = 12 \\
\times \qquad\qquad 4 \qquad \times 4 \\
\hline
4 \text{ tens } 8 \text{ ones} = 48
\end{array}
$$

b. Now, suppose that your child wants 16 chips on each of the 4 cupcakes. Help him discover the procedure is the same, except he will now have to regroup into new bundles of ten when using toothpicks, or write the new tens above the tens column in an algorithm.

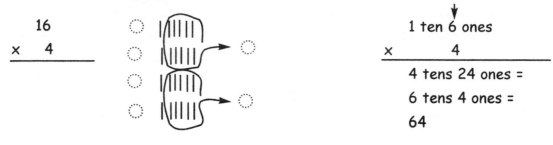

16
x 4
_____

1 ten 6 ones
x   4
_____
4 tens 24 ones =
6 tens 4 ones =
64

c. For calculations with two or more digits in the multiplier (36 x 24), show the procedure is the same except that a separate calculation is done for each digit.

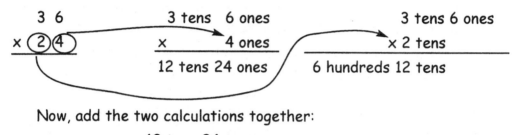

3 6
x (2)(4)

3 tens 6 ones
x   4 ones
_____
12 tens 24 ones

3 tens 6 ones
x 2 tens
_____
6 hundreds 12 tens

Now, add the two calculations together:

12 tens 24 ones
+ 6 hundreds 12 tens
_____
6 hundreds 24 tens 24 ones = 6 H 26 T 4 O = 8 H 6 T 40

By following these steps, your child now understands the process and knows the shorter algorithm for multiplication.

$$
\begin{array}{r}
1 \\
2 \\
36 \\
\times\ 24 \\
\hline
144 \\
72 \\
\hline
864
\end{array}
$$

5. Teaching Division:

Division is the opposite of multiplication. Your child has 64 marbles to divide equally among his 4 friends. He can give 1 bag of 10 marbles to each friend and then distribute the 24 single marbles. In division, unlike the other operations, the child must divide out the largest place values first. Many concrete sharing activities will establish the concept and process of division, preparing for the more abstract level.

a. To teach the calculation, begin with one of the practical experiences, such as the sharing of pennies, that will not require regrouping and divides by a single digit. Writing as you go, walk your child through the division process as you did for addition, subtraction, and multiplication. Start with the largest place values and share them out to the specified number of groups:

$$
\begin{array}{r}
2 \text{ tens} \\
\hline
4\,)\,86
\end{array}
$$

$$
\begin{array}{r}
2 \text{ tens} \\
\hline
4\,)\,8 \text{ tens } 6 \text{ ones} \\
-8 \text{ tens} \\
\hline
0 \text{ tens } 6 \text{ ones}
\end{array}
$$

- how many in each share in round 1?
- how many shared out in round 1?
- how many are left after round 1?

Now, move steadily toward the ones, as you continue to share:

$$
\begin{array}{r}
2 \text{ tens } 1 \text{ one} \\
\hline
4\,)\,8 \text{ tens } 6 \text{ ones} \\
-8 \text{ tens} \\
\hline
0 \text{ tens } 6 \text{ ones} \\
-4 \text{ ones} \\
\hline
2 \text{ ones}
\end{array}
$$

how many will each group get in round 2?
how many are shared out in round 2?
how many are left over?

b. For calculations needing regrouping, follow the same procedure.

$$
\begin{array}{r}
4 \overline{\smash{)}92}
\end{array}
\qquad
\begin{array}{r}
\text{2 tens 3 ones} \\
4 \overline{\smash{)}\text{9 tens 2 ones}} \\
\underline{-8 \text{ tens}} \\
\text{1 ten 2 ones} \\
\text{12 ones} \\
\underline{-12 \text{ ones}} \\
\text{0 ones}
\end{array}
\qquad
\begin{array}{r}
23 \\
4 \overline{\smash{)}92} \\
\underline{-80} \\
12 \\
\underline{-12} \\
0
\end{array}
$$

c. When dividing with a number of 2 digits or more, your child will be using the concepts of estimation and trial-and-error. Do not use toothpicks or marbles at this point; your child should now find a straightforward, paper calculation more manageable.

Encourage your child to ask himself questions to determine where to start, to estimate partial answers and to test them. Remind him the first estimate is not always correct, but will guide him to a more accurate second estimate.

$$
\begin{array}{r}
15 \\
36 \overline{\smash{)}542} \\
\underline{-36} \\
182 \\
\underline{-180} \\
2
\end{array}
$$

i) begin with the highest place value:

ii) for numbers which are not obvious, estimate:

  - will 6 work? Try it. ($36 \times 6 = 216$ - too big)
  - will 5 work? Try it. ($36 \times 5 = 180$ - yes!)

iii) continue to the end.

  - the answer is 15 with 2 remainder.

With division clear in your child's mind, you can be sure he now understands the place value system and knows the four essential arithmetic calculations. This is the basis of all later Math.

Some math facts should be memorized . . .

Memorization allows facts to be brought back immediately. This quick recall is important when your child is working with large-number calculations. Knowing the multiplication facts, she can then concentrate on the process, and not get hung-up on having to draw 9 groups of 6 or to look for the answer on a chart.

Memorizing facts may seem like an intimidating task. Take out much of the stress by showing your child how many he already knows. He probably knows that anything multiplied by zero is zero (both from concrete activities and from using a deductive approach). She knows that multiplying anything by 1 results in the same number she started with. He is probably familiar with the 2s, 5s, and 10s through skip-counting. Construct a multiplication chart with your child, guiding her to fill the facts she knows. Encourage him to watch for patterns as he develops the chart, noticing that all of the 10s end in zero, the 5s end in 5 or 0. What does he notice about a diagonal? Four adjacent cells? Suddenly, multiplication won't look quite so intimidating. By pointing out that each fact is written twice (7 x 6, 6 x 7) she will recognize that there aren't really that many to be learned after all. Half the battle has been won!

X	0	1	2	3	4	5	6	7	8	9	10
0	0	0	0	0	0	0	0	0	0	0	0
1	0	1	2	3	4	5	6	7	8	9	10
2	0	2	4	6	8	10	12	14	16	18	20
3	0	3	6			15					30
4	0	4	8			20					40
5	0	5	10	15	20	25	30	35	40	45	50
6	0	6	12			30					60
7	0	7	14			35					70
8	0	8	16			40					80
9	0	9	18			45					90
10	0	10	20	30	40	50	60	70	80	90	100

Memorization will happen incidentally as your child plays and works, but you can concentrate, as well, on embedding specific facts into games and activities each day.

Games, whether commercial or home-made, are fun for practicing facts. A game setting, with quick responses and the inherent quality of not always having to be right, causes less anxiety than working through a series of flash cards. Tossing dice or turning over cards allows for fun random questions. If you and your child make your own games, you can emphasize the specific facts which your child needs to practice. Use a variety of games and keep them fun!

Domino Bingo

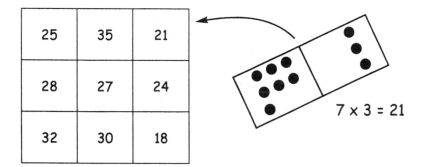

7 x 3 = 21

- Make bingo cards with at least three columns and three rows. Put addition or multiplication answers in each space.
- Turn dominoes for those facts upside down on the table.
- As each domino is turned up, cover the space which relates to it.
- The winner is the first person to cover 3 spaces in a line, vertically, horizontally, or diagonally.

Your Lucky Goal

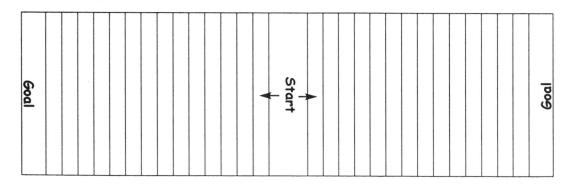

- Each player places his "puck" in the starting center square on a game board.

- The first player turns over an equation card (ex. 6 x 3 or 6 + 7).

- He calls out his answer and moves toward his goal on the left, moving only the number of "ones" in his answer. (6 x 3 = 18, so he moves 8 places to the left; 6 + 7 = 13 so he moves 3 places to the left.

- The next player calls out the answer for the next card, and moves toward his goal on the right.

- If an error is made, the player writes the correct equation on another paper, and then loses his turn. (The players can check their opponent's answers using a chart.)

Lucky Snake Eyes

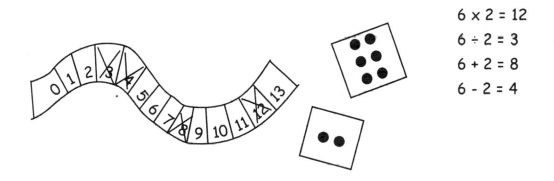

6 x 2 = 12

6 ÷ 2 = 3

6 + 2 = 8

6 - 2 = 4

- Each player makes his own game board with an agreed-upon number of spaces.

- The first player throws 2 die and adds, multiplies, subtracts and divides the two numbers shown. He covers up each of his answers on his game board. Who can cover his whole game board first?

War

- Distribute a regular deck of cards (Jack, Queen and King removed), among the players.

- Each player turns over 2 cards from his stack and the highest sum or product takes all.

- If there is a tie, WAR is declared and each player turns over another card adding it to their previous amount. Highest number wins all.

- The play continues until one player has collected all the cards.

  A version with dice:

- Each player throws 2 die, which are added or multiplied together.

- Highest number wins for each throw.

- Keep a tally with stones, marbles or pennies. The winner is the player who has the most objects in the tally.

Multiplication Rummy

- Players agree on what "table" they will be playing (ex. 8 times table)

- Deal 7 cards to each player, putting the remaining deck in the middle and turning up the top card. (The Joker is zero. Remove the J, K, and Q.)

- The first player takes either the face-up card or the top card from the deck. He then discards a card from his hand, placing it on top of the face-up card.

- At that time, he can lay down a card or two cards, to compose the digits of multiples of the agreed-upon table (for example, in the 8 times table game, he could lay down an 8, a 1 and 6 (i.e., 8 x 2 = 16), a 2 and 4, a 3 and 2, a 4 and Joker, a 4 and 8, a 5 and 6, a 6 and 4, and a 7 and 2).

- Play continues until one player wins that deal by laying all of his cards down.

Quick recall activities are fun for you and your child to design and make together. They're great to take along on a trip or to pull out for a spare moment (waiting for supper or a favorite T.V. show). If they are self-marking, an immediate response is provided.

Paper Plate Facts

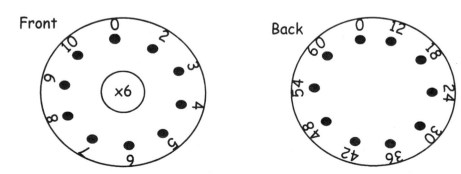

- Use a separate paper plate for each multiplication or addition table you wish to practice. For example, if the sixes need attention, write x 6 in the center of a plate, and other numbers around the plate edge.

- Punch holes beside these outside numbers, and write their corresponding answers (multiplying the center number with the outside number) next to the holes on the back of the plate.

- As your child answers each question, putting her pencil point into the appropriate hole, she turns the plate over, checking her response.

Triangular Facts

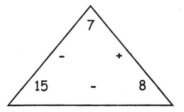

- Cut out triangles from cardboard. In one corner, write a sum (or product). In the other corners, write the addends that make up that sum.

- Hold the stack of triangles by a corner so that one numeral is always covered.

Physical activities involving numbers are especially valuable if your child learns best when his whole body is moving.

- skip-count by 3s while bouncing a ball or skipping rope

- play catch, calling out a question as you throw for her to catch as she answers

- hop the squares, calling out each answer as she hops into a square

| 7 x 6 | 7 x 3 | 4 x 7 | 8 x 7 |

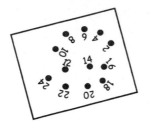 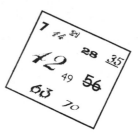

Combining art with Math provides an incentive for many children.

- find and color patterns on the addition and multiplication charts
- design number and fact posters
- create dot-to-dot pictures, using skip-counting

Music activities provide a rhythmic pattern with which to practice arithmetic facts.

- make facts part of a pattern – suggest a category, such as fraction equivalents or skip-counting and set it to rhythm (Children repeat the pattern rhythmically, slapping lap twice, clapping hands twice, and snapping fingers twice. On the snapping of the fingers, they add a fact to the category.)

> slap, slap, clap, clap, snap, snap "1/2"
> slap, slap, clap, clap, snap, snap "3/6"
>
> slap, slap, clap, clap, snap, snap "8"
> slap, slap, clap, clap, snap, snap "16"

- chant the multiplication tables
- make up rhyming couplets to incorporate facts ("5 times 5 is 25, now I think I'll take a dive")
- skip-count up the musical scales

12♩

10♩

8♩

6♩

4♩

2♩

Computer drills provide motivation for long periods of time. The best programs are those which give your child control. He should be able to input the facts he wants to work on, and to adjust the pace so that he can be successful. Be sure to check for these characteristics when considering video games. Computers are great in that your child suffers no loss of face if he makes a mistake. It is just between him and a machine. He can work at his own pace without feeling the need to please, or without outside pressure to "perform."

Tips and tidbits for teaching Math . . .

1. Watch for memory devices:

☞ Learning the multiplication facts for 9, point out that the two digits in each fact add up to 9:

$$3 \times 9 = 27 \ (2 + 7 = 9)$$
$$4 \times 9 = 36 \ (3 + 6 = 9)$$
$$5 \times 9 = 45 \ (4 + 5 = 9) \ \text{etc.}$$

☞ Memorize related addition and subtraction facts in groups, quartering the number of questions to be learned:

$$6 + 3 = 9 \qquad 3 + 6 = 9 \qquad 9 - 3 = 6 \qquad 9 - 6 = 3$$

☞ Memorize the multiplication and division facts together:

$$6 \times 3 = 18 \qquad 3 \times 6 = 18 \qquad 18 \div 3 = 6 \qquad 18 \div 6 = 3$$

☞ Have fun with Finger Multiplication (tables 6 through 9):

   a. point your fingers at each other palms down and label them as shown

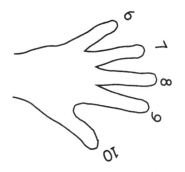
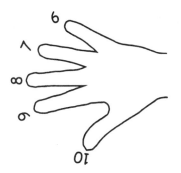

b. to solve an equation, such as 9 x 7, touch the tip of finger 9 on one hand to the tip of finger 7 on the other, keeping the palms down. Then fold under the thumbs and fingers of each hand which have numbers higher than the two which are touching.

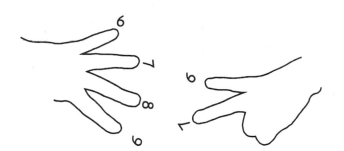

c. count by tens the number of pointing fingers (10, 20, 30, 40, 50, 60)

d. multiply the number of folded fingers of one hand by the folded fingers on the other hand (1 x 3 = 3)

e. add the 2 figures together (60 + 3 = 63)

2. Encourage your child to play "detective" while looking for patterns and developing their own rules:

6 x 0 = 0
4 x 0 = 0
0 x 3 = 0
0 x 9 = ?

5 x 1 = 5
7 x 1 = 7
1 x 9 = 9
1 x 8 = ?

5/6 x 3/4 = 15/24
5/8 x 1/2 = 5/16
2/3 x 4/5 = 8/15
6/7 x 2/3 = ?

5/6 - 2/6 = 3/6
4/8 - 1/8 = 3/8
2/5 - 1/5 = 1/5
4/7 - 2/7 = ?

(+3) x (-2) = -6
(+5) x (-3) = -15
(-4) x (+7) =-28
(+6) x (-8) = ?

3. Encourage your child to check his own work. Most students tend to rush to get an answer and then want to verify it with their teacher. Instead, ask him how he got his answer and why he thinks it's right. This enables him to review his own strategies and allows him to be more independent.

When adding numbers in a column, give your child different strategies to try. Add in the reversed direction. Group together doubles or watch for combinations of tens.

```
6 ⌐          6 ⌐          6 |          6 ↑
2 ⌐┘        ↗2 ⌐        2 |          2 |
4           (4 ⌐┘        4 |↓         4 |
8 ←        ↘8           8 ↓         8 |
───          ───          ───          ───
20           20           20           20
```

When subtracting, show your child how to check his work by adding his answer and the lower number to see if he gets what he started with:

$$\begin{array}{r} 36 \\ -\ 23 \\ \hline 13 \end{array} \qquad \begin{array}{r} 13 \\ +\ 23 \\ \hline 36 \end{array}$$

4. Using decimals:

When adding and subtracting decimal numbers, first line up the decimal points one under another. Then, line up the rest of the columns:

$$\begin{array}{r} 4.2 \\ +\ 36.54 \\ \hline 40.74 \end{array} \qquad \begin{array}{r} 36.2 \\ -\ .154 \\ \hline 36.354 \end{array}$$

When multiplying decimals, do the multiplication and then count up the decimal places in both the multiplier and multiplicand. Count the same number of places in your answer, from the right-hand side, and put in the decimal point:

$$\begin{array}{r} 3.6 \\ \times\quad .24 \\ \hline 144 \\ 72 \\ \hline .864 \end{array}$$

(3 decimal points)

(3 decimal points)

When dividing decimals, move the divisor's decimal point enough spaces to the right to make a whole number (no decimal point). Then, move the decimal point in the dividend the same number of spaces, adding zeros if necessary:

$$.62\,)\overline{1.534} \qquad 62\,)\overline{153.4}$$

5. Teaching Percentage: Use your basketball skills to initiate the meaning of percentage. Take turns having 10 tries each to make a basket. Record the number of makes and misses and compute the percentage of hits for each of you. 5/10 is 50/100 or 50%

   Per Cent means out of 100, so 60% is 60/100. If you need to find 60% of 90, calculate 60/100 x 90.

6. Money is a concrete version of our number system. Teaching place value, exchange pennies for dimes, dimes for dollars, dollars for ten-dollar bills, etc.

Hundreds	Tens	Ones
dollars	dimes	pennies

7. Integrate graphs into your daily activities. Graph rainfall, grocery bills, birds at your bird feeder, etc. The organization of data is an important skill.

My Family's Shoes			
	✓		
	✓		
✓	✓		
✓	✓		✓
✓	✓		✓
✓	✓	✓	✓
Velcro	Lace-up	Buckle	Slip-on

8. Teach Geometry with toothpicks and plasticene. Make shapes, explore perimeter, area, and volume, design complex structures.

Use the environment. Measure and calculate the perimeter and area of their rooms, the garage, their Lego construction, etc.

9. Teaching Fractions:

Go for a fraction walk, pointing out examples of fractions in your environment. How many windows does your house have? How many of those are on the side facing the street? Notice parts in a whole – panels on a door, trees on a street, posts on a fence, doors on a car, etc.

A hierarchy for teaching fraction operations:

Addition	Subtraction
a. 3 + 7/10	a. 9/10 - 5/10
b. 2/5 + 1/5	b. 3 7/10 - 3/10
c. 3/10 + 7/10	c. 4 - 5/10
d. 3/4 + 3/4	d. 7/10 - 1/2
e. 4 2/3 + 1 2/3	e. 2 1/2 - 9/10
f. 1/2 + 3/10	f. 4 1/5 - 2 7/10
g. 2 1/2 + 1 9/10	

Multiplication	Division
a. 4 x 1/2	a. 2 ÷ 1/3
b. 1/2 x 1/2	b. 1/3 ÷ 2
c. 3 1/2 x 1/2	c. 3/4 ÷ 1/4
d. 3 1/2 x 4 1/5	d. 4 1/2 ÷ 1/2
	e. 4/5 ÷ 1 3/5
	f. 2 2/3 ÷ 1 1/3
	g. 3 ÷ 1 1/2
	h. 1 1/2 ÷ 3

Chapter 5

How to weave writing into your day . . .

Your child began to write with his first mark on a foggy window. He made an impression, or rather an expression, by tracing with his finger. When he drew his first picture with his sister's bright red marker, he experienced the permanency of his ideas. As he added random letters, then letters relating to sounds, then words and finally stories, he was putting his thoughts onto paper. He could now hold on to his ideas, share them, revisit them, extend them or rearrange them. This is writing! Join in his enthusiasm! Just as your child learned to talk by talking, walk by walking, ride his bike by riding, so he learns to write by writing.

1. Be alert to writing opportunities

Help your child to develop his skill in writing by giving him many opportunities to practice. Weave writing into your everyday life, showing him how useful it is. As you take phone messages or write self-reminders, make grocery lists or plan your day, he will begin to recognize ways that writing serves his needs as well. A bulletin board will motivate your family to communicate with each other through messages and ideas or jokes and riddles. Johnny may want to give his dad a wish-list, remind himself to return his library books, or put up a warning, "Don't open Crackles' cage!" Encourage Justine to jot notes of how her family can make her new dog feel at home. James' friend may ask for a list of steps for tying fishing flies.

Grasp any situation to encourage writing. Charts or observation lists can be kept in the barn, near the bird feeder, or by the garden. Cooking recipes can be exchanged, and jingles written for favorite cereals. Words for songs can be added to her composition at the piano. Have fun with writing, and let it be an integral part of your child's day.

Revitalize letter-writing, but let him write real letters to real people for real reasons. Joey could invite his cousin or pen pal for a visit or tell him about his snowboard trip. A family co-operative letter is a great way to include everyone's message to Grandma. Help Jimmy find an address to write to (Government or mining company office), asking for information about the rock-layering he noticed. Brian might need to write to the Mexican consulate to learn more about the customs and holidays of Mexico. Adolescence is a time of causes – your teenager might like to express his opinion in the local paper, or write to members of Government to take a stand on an issue.

Writing letters can also motivate writing in a journal. Set aside time each evening for your child to record his feelings, his accomplishments and the events of the day – a great source to refer to when writing his to pen pal. Younger children can draw a picture on half the page, writing a sentence about a particularly good or bad thing that happened that day. Be sure that you, too, write entries in your journal, even if it's only a few observations on how the learning went. Following your model, your child will find journal writing not only a useful reference, but an opportunity to organize thoughts onto paper – a time for reflection.

The events of your day will suggest many incidental writing activities; just be sure to encourage writing at every occasion.

2. Stir in some creative writing

Story-writing begins with your young child's first drawings. Be his scribe, writing the story he tells as he talks about his picture, printing from left to right, top to bottom. Later he will imitate your work by making his own marks, using "wavy line writing," and then will read back his own story as he follows the lines with his finger. Without realizing it, he is seeing how print reflects the world around him. As he learns some of the letters and sounds, he will begin to insert them into his lines. Soon he will be printing whole words and sentences, as they sound. This is an exciting development for both him and you. He has truly begun to express his ideas by writing. Celebrate his stories and encourage him to share them with others.

Children use different strategies as they compose their stories. Some days, she may begin writing immediately, while at other times, talking predominates. Encourage her to jot down her ideas while she talks, extending her thinking by asking for more details or how she feels about it. Spelling isn't essential for brainstorming, but if spelling words correctly is important to her at this time, quickly write down the ideas as she relays them. She then has a vocabulary to refer to when she begins writing her story in earnest and won't be hampered by her concern for "correctness." Your child may think best while drawing, adding visual details as he develops his idea. Or he may enjoy dramatizing, becoming the character for his story, developing a plot as he reacts. Watch what works for him and give him space to be openly creative, but schedule a block of time each day to get into the rhythm of this process. We learn to write by writing, and we need the time to write.

Your child's stories may develop from her everyday activities, or from a world of her own where things only exist in the mind. She may enjoy revisiting her favorite books; they are ideal as models for the framework of her own stories. The patterns and repetitions of "Three Billy Goats Gruff" can structure a similar story. The cumulative details of "The House That Jack Built" can set the challenge for keeping a story building to its very end. Problem-centered stories, such as "Rumplestiltskin," will help her to develop a story moving from a problem to a plan and finally to a solution. Your child can look for examples of good beginnings and endings, of strong descriptions and of ways suspense is created in the books she enjoys. Have her ask herself how the author gets her interested or excited.

If she's fallen in love with poetry, bring it out! Have fun with rhymes and chants while skipping rope. Write them down as poems. Join her as she sings her favorite songs, emphasizing the beat and rhyme. It's fun to create "Piggy-back" songs together, putting her own words to familiar tunes. For example, Sarah might enjoy substituting "Do you know the astronaut, the astronaut, the astronaut" to the Muffin Man song. Older children will benefit from experimenting with different forms and rhythms in poetry and will enjoy developing vivid images with you.

Your child can be inspired to write creatively by varying the size and type of papers and by providing different writing tools – a calligraphy pen for a descriptive passage, bright felt pens for informative posters, a paintbrush with black ink to write haiku. Encourage her to explore ideas, methods and materials. She will enjoy creating her own booklets (scribe them if necessary), illustrating and binding them, and sharing them with friends. A computer word-processing program will create a professional "look" and can motivate reluctant writers.

Write alongside your child whenever possible, letting her know exactly what you're doing and how you're solving problems of composition. Share her enthusiasm for stories to be told!

Most of all, your child needs an audience for his writing, so listen to him and ask him questions. Laugh, smile, cry, nod or sigh, but let him see that his message matters, that you enjoyed his story.

3. Develop skills of report writing

Be alert to your child's surprises and discoveries. Share Ashley's enthusiasm as she bubbles with delight, eager to describe and learn more about the "skater bug" she saw skimming across the pond's surface. Writing a report allows her to become an expert, sharing her interest and knowledge with others. Her report has relevance. Now is the time to check out a nature address on the Internet, head to the library to gather books and magazines about pond life, visit the nature center, or interview an older friend who is interested in insects.

Saturated with enthusiasm and information, she can now organize her thoughts, recognizing that she has something important to say. Show her how to brainstorm, jotting down thoughts as they come up, and then grouping these ideas with different colored felt pens (as you notice a couple of ideas about its habitat, you could circle them both with green; when a few ideas emerge regarding appearance, they could be circled in blue, etc.). When she sees that many of her ideas can be grouped together, she can arrange them in a cluster map (sometimes called a mind map or spider map), using categories which work for her. She can then use this map as the paragraph structure to write her report. The example below uses the standard "how," "why," "when," "where" and "what" categories. She could just as easily group her ideas into "habitat," "habits," life cycle" and "appearance" or into other categories which would best cover her information.

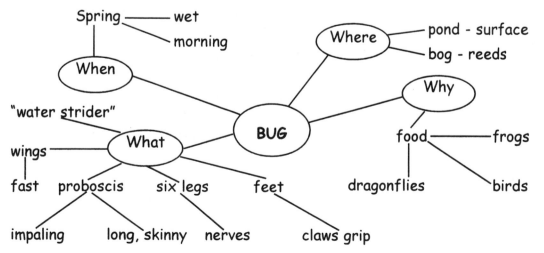

Other strategies for organizing ideas can be developed – writing outlines, setting up flow charts, moving from the most important characteristic to the least or supporting a statement with details. She may try different introductions to her report – relating an anecdote, composing an intriguing description, stating a startling fact or asking a question. She may focus on a specific item, or write about skaters in relation to other pond creatures. Introduce these strategies and watch to see which work best for her. Encourage her to continue experimenting with new ideas and methods.

When your child is finished the draft, take a break. Later, ask her to listen to herself as she reads it aloud, checking that each item really does relate to her topic and that she has told her audience all she wanted to say. Encourage her to present her report as an expert on water striders!

Whenever possible, your child should write about what interests him. He could follow up on a newspaper article about Michael Jordan, or write about a favorite holiday in Mexico or choose race-car driving. If a school report has been assigned, help him focus on a specific aspect which grabs his attention. Build up background on the topic by watching a video together, looking at pictures from a magazine, borrowing inspiring books, talking with experts in the field or having fun with a related art activity. His enthusiasm will grow as you become enthusiastic yourself! Encourage him to begin gathering impressions and information immediately, while the assignment is fresh in his mind. He can then take the time to explore the topic, making it his own.

4. Provide strategies for proofreading and editing

Practice is as important in writing as it is in throwing hoops in basketball, working on spirals in figure skating or learning the multiplication facts. To make him want to practice writing, your child must meet success. He must feel safe while trying new words and new techniques. As he writes, point out an effective phrase he has used or a specific verb or an exciting beginning. Edit from a positive angle, showing him the value of his work. It is important to accept his ideas and not to discourage his explorations by continually marking up his writing with corrections in mechanics or spelling.

Instead, provide her with strategies to do her own editing and proofreading. When she is ready to rework a favorite piece of writing, have her reread it aloud to herself and to you, taking the time to rethink it, to re-talk about it, and to experiment with it. Ask her questions about what she likes about her article, what she thinks works and which areas, if any, are bothering her. Show her new ways to present her information, rearranging the sentences or trimming or linking them together. Comment on specific verbs she used, such as "crept" instead of "walked quietly," or the way she carved a clear image with sensory impressions. Show her how to cross out for deletions, use arrows for insertions, and cut and paste to rearrange, so she doesn't need to rewrite for each change. Let her take control of her writing, but listen to her talk as she makes changes and watch her strategies, helping her to take them to the next level. Even at this critical stage, her writing must be appreciated and treated with respect.

Now that he sees how easily his writing can be reshaped, take this opportunity to teach mechanics as they are needed, finding solutions and examples in a good grammar guide. Use a light touch, mentioning only one or two items at each editing. You can make a note of other areas that need work and return to them at a later time.

As you discuss specific grammar, punctuation and capitalization skills, add them to a checklist for your child to refer to while proofreading. This list will change as your child's writing becomes more sophisticated. When she no longer needs a specific reminder, omit it from the list, adding new skills as they come up in her writing.

✓	Began each sentence with a capital letter
	Used quotation marks around what somebody said
✓	Used a question mark at the end of questions
✓	Used a period at the end of sentences
✓	Included a subject and verb in every sentence
	. . .
	. . .

Learning to write with good spelling takes time. It's important that you believe and trust that good spelling will develop as your child continues to write and read. He will pick up spelling patterns and sound-symbol relationships with experience. You can help him to become more aware of patterns by pointing them out as they come up in his daily writing. Look for roots, suffixes and prefixes, relating what is new to what is already known. Let him see you try out different spellings as you write, looking to see which appears correct, then always checking with a dictionary. Gradually, he can build up his own dictionary (a notebook with one page for each letter of the alphabet), filling in correctly spelled words as he learns them. Knowing how to spell one word often leads to the correct spelling of many words with similar patterns or with other prefixes or suffixes, so his dictionary will build up quickly. His writing vocabulary will increase, his confidence grow, and his proofreading will be more effective.

Many times, your child will want to write just to get her ideas down, to create a pool from which to draw. These rough compositions are important in themselves, and should not be weighed down by heavy editing. Using a two-sided portfolio, the rough compositions can be placed in one pocket – a treasure chest to which to refer when writing a piece to share with others. The polished writing can be dated and placed in the second pocket. Both types of composition are important and should each be recognized for their special qualities. Provide many opportunities to write but only expect some of the stories, reports and poems to be edited and brought to a "finished" stage (about one in five).

Tips and Tidbits for learning phonics

- When your child first shows interest in letter and sound connections, gradually introduce the letters one or two at a time, forming them with play dough or tracing them in sand as he hears and says the sounds the letters make. Together, think of words beginning with those sounds.

- Together, collect magazine pictures beginning with a specific letter. Collect examples of the letter from large print on cereal boxes, magazine headings, etc. Use the letters and pictures to design letter posters and display them around the room, adding to them throughout the days.

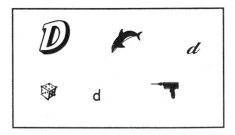 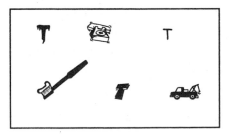

- Play with rhymes (the fat cat had a bat) and alliterative phrases (creepy creatures crawl carefully) to develop a sharp awareness in hearing different sounds.

- Match puzzles relating letter sounds with words or pictures (commercial or home-made)

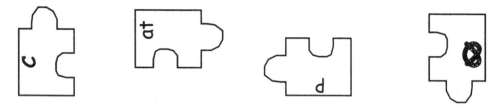

- Hop to letter sounds (or skip or jump, or touch your toes, or any action).

- Play Sidewalk Hopscotch, calling out the letter you hop into, or words beginning with the letter you land on. Later, print suffixes or prefixes in the squares, requiring the hopper to call out words using those suffixes or prefixes.

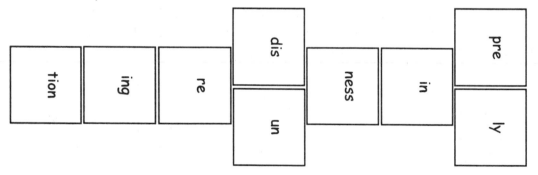

- Play word games, such as "I Spy," with initial letters ("I spy something that is red and starts with 't'") and later, final letters ("I spy something that is red and ends with 'p'"). These short games are great for spare moments, or while waiting at the doctor's office, or while driving in a car.

- Word-construction games, such as Scrabble and Boggle, encourage the whole family to enjoy playing with words.

- Some children like to use commercial phonics and printing books, playing school.

- If your child is at the writing stage, but continues to have difficulty sounding out words as he writes his stories, note the specific difficulties, and at another time, explore the letter-sound relationships again, using the multi-sensory techniques above.

Tips and Tidbits for Spelling

☛ As your child learns a few letters, you can help her spell words by:

a. showing an object that corresponds to a simple phonetic word - "cat"

b. "What is the first sound you hear? Write it in the first space" _C_ ___ ___

c. "What is the last sound you hear? Write it at the end" _C_ ___ _t_

d. "What do you hear in the middle? Write it in the middle. " _C_ _a_ _t_

☛ **Some tricks to learn spelling:**

ear/hear/heard	knowledge on the ledge
here/there/where	their/heir
Ted was led to bed.	head was heavy as lead
three weeks	eat meat
piece of pie	too soon
wise to advise	advice to mice
owl is a fowl	throw seeds to sow

☛ **Have fun constructing word families with your child:**

Cut two strips of paper, making slots in one strip to weave the other strip through. Print a familiar "ending" on the "slots" strip.

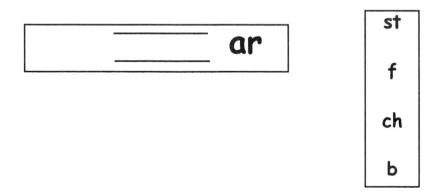

On the weaving strip, write letters which will compose words when joined with the "ending."

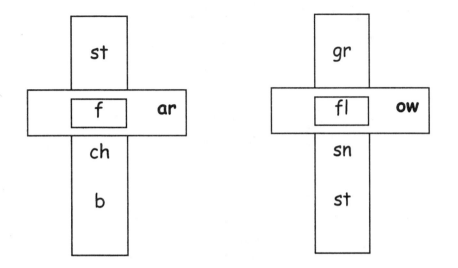

Chapter 6

How to instill the joy of reading . . .

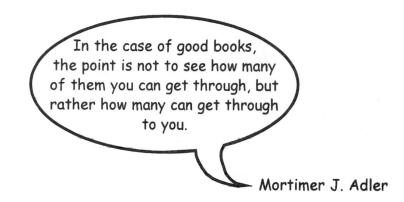

In the case of good books, the point is not to see how many of them you can get through, but rather how many can get through to you.

— Mortimer J. Adler

A successful reader is a reader who loves to read and who reads often. Your goal will be to instill this love of reading in your child. Let him experience reading as an enjoyable activity, something he will want to do. Reading is a skill that builds on itself. The more it is practiced, the easier it becomes, so he reads even more.

Share your joy in books by reading to your child many times throughout the day, even if only for short periods.

The stories will come alive as you emphasize exciting words and adopt character voices, varying your reading in volume and speed. By choosing books you both enjoy, you can interact honestly with your child, reacting together to the characters and events.

Running your finger under the words you read aloud, you indicate the left to right movement of print without even commenting. Sometimes, phrases can be swept together and at other times, individual words can be tracked. Your child will begin to recognize words which keep cropping up, particularly if there are repetitions, rhyming words, or predictable patterns. Soon, she will be leaping in to join you. Discovery is an exciting part of learning. She has discovered that she can read words herself! She can help you move a bookmark, placing it above the line you are reading, tracking the print, yet still looking ahead.

As well as reading familiar phrases and rhymes together, have fun taking character parts while enjoying a favorite story. Or share a book by reading alternate sentences aloud, or paragraphs or even chapters. If the material is difficult, he might prefer to read a sentence for each page you read. This not only keeps the story flowing, but often words will reoccur and provide familiarity.

If your child reads haltingly, word by word, echo reading will force her eyes to move more quickly. Reading at a pace slightly faster than hers, with natural phrasing, encourage her to read along with you, keeping up as well as she can. She will begin to look at groups of words as she absorbs the meaning of the complete passage.

Even after he is reading well on his own, don't stop reading to your child. A bedtime story is an opportunity for relaxing and enjoying books together. By sharing different types of books, you are building his vocabulary and his pool of knowledge and as you read a topic of your choice, you introduce new interests. Include difficult reading materials, as well. A child's level of understanding is several levels above his ability to read. He will appreciate more intricate details and more complex ideas and be challenged to follow up on his own.

The importance of one-to-one story sharing cannot be emphasized enough. As well, however, take young children to story time at the library or arrange group sessions with other families. This social interaction allows for different emotions and ideas, as each responds to the story in his own way.

Model the habit of reading. Let your child see you read to yourself, both for pleasure and for information.

Children have never been very good at listening to their elders, but they have never failed to imitate them.

— James Baldwin

By scheduling a time each day for the whole family to read independently, you are providing models and establishing an important routine. This is a great time for Dad to read the newspaper or the novel he borrowed. You can escape with your favorite author, or catch up on an article in a magazine. Maria will enjoy looking through her picture books or listening to a story on the tape recorder with ear phones. Brian may be learning about Mexican celebrations while David disappears into another of his Hardy Boys books. Charlene may want to revisit her home-made booklets or favorite stories from her writing portfolio. Provide a varied selection of reading material, being sure the books you shared together are available as well.

Incorporate reading into the day's events. Whether it be checking television schedules, reading street signs or looking for more information on water striders, your child will become aware that reading is useful. Justine can learn how to train her new puppy. Chelsey can follow a favorite muffin recipe. Jeremy can check off directions while making his kite. Many reading activities occur spontaneously, but watch for occasions to slip in even more! Try writing notes or posting messages on the bulletin board . . . "Help yourself to cookies in the refrigerator, Janine." "I was out looking at your carrots today – do you want to dig some up for supper?" "I left some wood kite strips in the garage, Jeremy."

Help your child acquire the strategies of a good reader. Skills will evolve naturally as your child reads and writes. You can help her to become an even more proficient reader by following various strategies.

Good readers read fluently, with confidence. By giving your child reading material he is comfortable with, he can practice the skill of fluent reading. His own written or scribed books have familiar content and vocabulary and will be easy for him to read. Pattern books with repeated phrases (such as Henny Penny telling all her friends that "The sky is falling down") are quickly grasped and followed. Provide occasions for him to reread favorite stories over and over again, on a tape recorder, to his brother or dog, over the telephone. Each time, he will acquire more and more confidence in his skill as a reader.

Help your child choose books which relate to his experiences, encouraging him to make connections by identifying with the characters and events. A book about Wayne Gretzky will inspire your hockey-playing son to read a much more difficult book than usual. He will be able to predict words and follow the content as he reads for information he needs. Building his backyard fort, Devon might find some handy tips from deciphering the picture captions in a construction magazine of his dad's. Wanting more information on Saturn, Sarah's brother might skim through the National Geographic magazines. Reading levels leap when the content is meaningful and interesting!

Older children may find that reading silently will keep the story and ideas flowing. Continue to discuss his reading with him, however. Ask what he thinks the story will be about before he begins, making predictions from picture clues, and from the table of contents or chapter titles. Later, he may enjoy retelling the story by drawing or writing the events on a sectioned strip of paper. He might use puppets to re-enact it. These activities help with comprehension, summarizing and sequencing the ideas.

Many readers find that reading aloud helps them to understand the print better. Don't worry if she omits or substitutes a word as long as it doesn't change the meaning. A good reader often skips over unfamiliar words, returning to them when he knows the rest of the sentence.

If the content of the rest of the sentence doesn't help identify a word through its meaning, encourage her to try other strategies for deciphering. Try looking at the first letter or blend, using the phonics she practiced while writing and spelling. Whispering the first consonant may be the only clue she needs! A longer word might require a middle or end consonant. Check it for roots, suffixes, or prefixes. Don't worry about sounding the whole word out. A few letters, along with the meaning of the sentence, will most often "spark" the word. If she still hesitates, tell her the word and let the reading continue. Jot the difficulty down and return to it later in a more familiar context, isolating it from that reading experience.

Many words are difficult to read by "sounding them out," yet your child will meet them over and over again (could, play, because, etc.). With lots of exposure, he will begin to recognize them by sight. Give practice in identifying these frequently-used words by playing games as you search for and highlight them in newspapers or magazines. Toss a large home-made die, reading the sight word that faces up, or play a memory game by pairing word cards which have been scattered upside down. Call out the words as you hop into the hopscotch squares or see them flashed on the computer screen. By recognizing these words quickly, he will be able to skim through them as he reads, grasping the larger ideas presented without having to decipher each word.

If she is having difficulty with reading, be patient and positive, recognizing each success along the way. As she explores books and acquires skills and strategies through practice, she is establishing a solid foundation for reading. Learning happens in spurts, and each step needs time for consolidation. Your one-to-one individual attention will provide a real advantage.

Let reading be fun and books be friends. Your child will discover that books can amuse him when he wants to laugh, help him when he needs instruction, stimulate him when he wants to think, and comfort him when he needs reassurance. Give him lots of pleasurable time to interact with books. Encourage him to reread his favorites in different ways, playing with them, acting them out, designing covers and title pages, composing fun dedications, using them as models to create his own stories, devouring them. He will do this as he internalizes your enthusiasm.

Be sure to visit the public library often, browsing and gathering books to share and to read independently. As he receives gift books, he will build up his own library with books he can turn to time and time again. Reading will be a favorite "subject" in your Kitchen Table Classroom. The skills will develop as the reading happens.

Tips and Tidbits for Reading

- ☛ **Create a visual representation** of how much your child reads. It could be a necklace to which you add one bead for each story she reads, cardboard keys to add to a large ring, circles to develop a caterpillar which encircles his room, or any other idea which would motivate your child. A very successful plan for Chelsea was to collect macaroni noodles on a long piece of wool, adding a bead for each tenth "reading." Be sure to recognize home-made booklets and books read over and over again, as well, because these have much value. If your representation permits, include the book title and author on each section, so he can look back to see the books he enjoyed, not just how many.

☞ **Word jigsaws** are fun to make and play. Print a familiar nursery rhyme or poem on a large sheet of paper, making a copy on a smaller card. Help your child to cut up the large print into sentence strips to be scattered and then rearranged in the correct order, reconstructing the poem. Later, cut the strips into words for an even greater challenge.

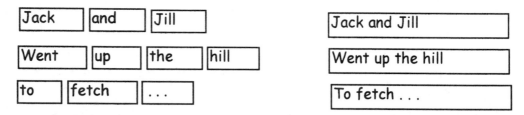

☞ **Word Toss** – Print a "sight" word on each side of home-made cubes. Toss the dice and call out the word that faces up.

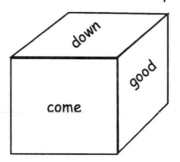

☞ **Sight Memory Games** – Print duplicate sight word cards and scatter them upside down on a table. Each person has three tries to turn over pairs, reading each card as he does so. If he gets a pair, he keeps them. The trick is to remember where each card is. The person who gathers the most pairs wins the Memory Game.

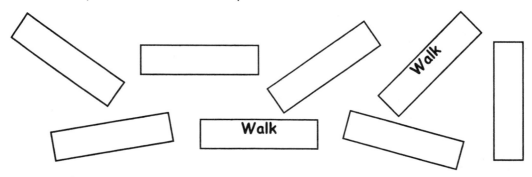

Sight words to practice in games:

come	down	some
here	look	walk
play	said	the
where	you	call
are	when	good
have	like	were
our	please	saw
say	there	they
because	want	was
what	who	buy
away	again	could
know	does	put
right	their	wash
would	done	hurt
warm	together	try

Chapter 7

How to stir in additional subject areas . . .

Let the world be the extension of your "Kitchen Table Classroom." As your child explores, he is constantly learning. You can tap into his inquisitive nature, sharing his curiosity and observations as he makes discoveries in Science and Social Studies and as he experiments with techniques of Art.

Arrange for field trips to pursue particular interests as you explore your neighborhood together. Fish hatcheries, nature centres, astronomical observatories, construction sites, caves, forests, swamps, creeks, museums, exhibits, government offices, art galleries, ethnic stores, historical sites and architecturally interesting buildings are just a few of the many opportunities to learn from your environment. Watch for occasions to visit with professionals in their related fields. Often, park officials will advertise a lecture on bats or local plants or spawning salmon. A museum curator will be happy to discuss the extinction of dinosaurs or the culture of the local First Nations group. Geologists can be contacted to help with rock and mineral identification. Follow up the interests of older children by providing experiences in life skills and career preparation - apprenticing with a carpenter, plumber, electrician, car mechanic or construction company, or taking specific courses in forestry management or computer programming, or volunteering in a health facility or home for the elderly. "School" is not a place to memorize, but rather to experience, to think, to see relationships and to draw conclusions.

This chapter suggests a variety of activities to help in your quest for ideas. Incorporate them as your child shows an interest, or use them as inspiration to spark a theme.

Some practical science suggestions your child may enjoy:

Have Fun Gardening

A producing garden is a perfect opportunity to integrate many learning activities – measuring the height of plants, reading instructions for planting and watering, designing landscape patterns, recognizing plant and soil needs, selling produce, accepting responsibilities. If you have space, hand over a garden area for your child to plant her own flowers and vegetables without interference. A narrow raised bed is ideal. She can weed and water around the circumference, without having to walk through the plants. Large seeds such as pumpkins, peas and nasturtiums are easy for young children to handle. Cosmos and marigolds grow quickly to keep her interest sustained. Strawberries and carrots provide a tasty reward. But let your child make her own choices and let the garden be hers. Only through experience do we learn and grow.

Grow some sprouts in a jar

- Put 2 tablespoons of seeds (Alfalfa, cabbage, mung beans, etc.) in a large, wide-mouthed jar. Cover the jar with a double layer of cheese-cloth and secure with a rubber band.
- Fill half the jar with water and let it stand overnight.
- Pour out the water through the cheesecloth. Then turn the jar several times to spread the moist seeds over its inner surface. Rinse the seeds with water through the cheesecloth two or three times a day, each time re-spreading the seeds. (They need to be moist but not wet.) Sprouts need light to grow, but direct sunlight will dry them out.
- After about 4 days, discard the cheesecloth and eat the sprouts.
- Discuss what sprouts need to grow. Compare the look and taste of 3-day-old sprouts to that of 5-day-old sprouts.

Make a pop bottle greenhouse

- Cut the top off a 2-liter clear plastic pop bottle, using scissors.
- Turn the bottle on its side and lay it in a pan with crushed newspaper around it so it won't roll.
- Place some stones in the bottom, and then a layer of soil about 5 cm thick.

- Plant some seeds or plants in the soil and add just enough water to dampen.
- Fasten plastic wrap around the open end with a rubber band.
- Place your greenhouse where it will get some sun, but not be too hot.
- Discuss how the garden will get watered. (As the greenhouse warms up, the water in the soil evaporates. That water vapor collects on the inside of the plastic bottle and falls back as rain.)

Check out seeds

- Gather seeds in the fall and, using your "detective" skills, determine how they travel from place to place. The seeds could be dispersed as parachute-like puffs (milkweed, dandelion, cattails), with helicopter-like wings (maple, linden, ash), by floating on water (coconut, cranberry), by being catapulted through expulsion (peas, jewelweed, violets), by hitching a ride using burrs and hooks, or by being deposited after animals and birds have eaten their fruits.
- Cut several types of fruit in half, between the stem and blossom end and compare the patterns and numbers of seeds in the fruit halves.
- Make seed rattles by putting seeds in margarine containers, comparing the sounds of the different seeds as you shake the rattles.

Learn About Animals

Pets provide a great opportunity for children to learn about and take responsibility for animals. Or make frequent visits to a farm or petting zoo to watch the hatching of chicks or the growth of a colt. If you are unable to have a pet in your home, your child might enjoy volunteering at the S.P.C.A. or other service which cares for animals.

Make a bird-feeding station

- Cut out 1/2 of one side of a large plastic milk jug (don't cut off top or bottom).
- Cut a hole under the front of the opening for a stick to fit in as a perch.
- Attach a string and hang your feeder in a safe place, out of reach of cats and other animals.

- Put seeds in the feeder, hang suet and apples near the feeder in a mesh bag (an onion bag is great), and set out a pan of water nearby.
- Graph the number and types of birds which visit your bird-feeding station.

Create a pond in a jar

- Lay 2 cm. of bottom mud on the bottom of a large jar (washed thoroughly without detergents).
- Carefully, pour pond water down the side of the jar (about 3/4 full) taking care not to disturb the bottom.
- Add a few pond plants (and freshly-laid frog eggs if you like) and a stick, leaning against the inside of the jar, long enough to extend out of the water.
- Place the jar carefully by a north-facing window, monitoring it so that it doesn't overheat.
- Check your ecosystem every day to watch for changes in the populations of small invertebrates. Using a reference book and a magnifying glass, see if you can identify any of the creatures.
- Watch out for:
    - overheating – everything dies and turns black
    - lack of oxygen – everything gradually turns orange, and then black
    - no light – the walls of the jar become covered in black or brown diatoms. Scrape them off to let the light in.
- When finished, return the components to their original source. Discuss the interdependence of pond life.

Make a desert terrarium

- Wash a large jar or aquarium.
- Place a layer of coarse gravel over the bottom and cover it with dry sand.
- Plant small cactus plants in the sand, covering the roots completely.
- Place a small pan of water in a corner.
- Cover your terrarium with wire screening and put it in or near a window where it will not receive direct sunlight
- Water the plants once every three weeks.

- Study lizards or snakes in your terrarium, providing them with water and food (ants, houseflies, grasshoppers or worms). Be sure to release them outside after a day or so.

Create a marsh environment

- Place a block of wood under one end of your terrarium so that it is on a slant.
- Spread a layer of gravel at the upper of end of the slant and cover the gravel with rich, moist soil and moss, ferns, and other marsh plants.
- Pour water into the lower end of the terrarium until it meets the soil.
- Cover your terrarium with a piece of window glass and place it near or in a window where it does not receive direct sunlight.
- Add snails, salamanders, turtles or frogs for short periods. For food, include lettuce leaves, insects, fruit flies, overripe fruit, earthworms.

Check out frozen soil

- Dig up a piece of solidly frozen surface soil from a field or wood lot and put it in a clear glass jar.
- Cover your jar with window glass and put it in a warm sunny window, checking it out after a couple of days.

Build a nature blind

- Tack or staple parallel wood stakes to a large piece of burlap.
- Cut a window in the center of each burlap "wall," at a comfortable height.
- Hammer the stakes into the ground so that the burlap stands up and stretches tight.
- Spray paint brown spots to camouflage the burlap.
- Set up your blind near a pond of water or in an area where you have noticed animals before. Silence and a lack of movement will help to make your viewing successful.
- When you've finished viewing, pull out the stakes and roll up the blind, tying it with string for easier carrying to your next observation site.

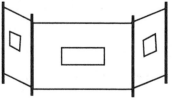

Make an insect zoo

- Capture a few insects from a single area.
- Place them, along with some leaves and soil, in a large, wide-mouthed, glass jar.
- Cover your jar with netting or nylon stocking, securing it with an elastic band.
- Keep these insects for only a short time, giving you a close-up view, and then return to their natural environment.

Set up an ant colony in a jar

- Put a lid on a small jar and place this inside a larger jar.
- Scoop a group of ants from one hill of loose earth. Include the queen (bigger than the other ants), some soil, white eggs and larvae. Place them into the space between the small and large jar. Leave your mixture loose, unpacked down.
- Keep a moist (not wet) piece of sponge on top of the small jar at all times and use a spray bottle every day to keep the soil slightly moist.
- Provide a little food, experimenting with different kinds (overeating will kill the ants; one drop of honey will feed 50 ants for a week).
- Cover the large jar with nylon stocking, securing it with an elastic band.
- Tape black paper around the outside of the jar so that the ants will tunnel close to the glass. Keep in a dim cool place.
- After a few days, remove the black paper, observing the ants using dim light.
- If the ants are making new tunnels, they are happy and you can replace the black paper until the next time you want to observe. Any other activity means that they should be returned to their natural habitat.
- Once the ant colony is established, you might like to bring in an ant from another hill and observe the interaction.

Explore the Earth

Notice rock cuts along the side of a road or railroad.
- Look for layering of various rock types.

- Look for folding and fault offsets of the layers, showing earth movements.

- Recreate these rock cuts using plasticene.

- Simulate the natural process of sedimentation by adding a handful of sand to a large jar of water each day, letting it settle. Try to obtain two or three types of sand of differing color or grain. If the different sands are used on alternate days, each day's contribution will appear as a discrete sedimentary bed. Occasionally add some small pebbles to show how a conglomerate is made.

Visit a gravel pit

- Look for signs of layered glacial deposits, including till layers, stream layers of sand and gravel, and glacial lake layers of thin-bedded mud and silts.

- Look for pieces of trees and other ice-age plants preserved in the deposits.

Simulate erosion

- Build a little mountain, incorporating different soils and hard and soft clay areas. Sprinkle water on top with a watering can to simulate rain, and notice how the soft areas are eroded away. Discuss other causes of erosion (wind, ice) and watch for examples in the environment.

Look for signs of former volcanic activity in the rocks

- You might find layers of volcanic ash or other material (pumice balls or glass shards) which had been blown out of a volcanic vent.

- You might find pieces of glassy obsidian, caused when magma cools very quickly.

- You might find lava pillows, caused when magma cools quickly as it plunges into water, forming pillow-shaped structures in the rock.

Recreate your own volcano

- Build a mountain of dirt, sand, clay, or plasticene about a foot high.

- Bury a small jar with a wide neck in the top of your mountain with the opening sticking out.

- Put 4 tablespoons of baking soda in the small jar.

- Mix 1/2 cup water, 1/4 cup dish washing liquid, 1/4 cup white vinegar and a few drops of red food coloring in a large container.
- Pour some of the mixture into the small jar to create an eruption.

Collect rocks and minerals

- Gather a variety of specimens as you hike in your area, trying to find samples which have single minerals and others which have combinations of minerals.
- Separate your specimens into two categories – rocks and minerals (rocks contain a number of minerals).
- Refer to a clearly illustrated book or field guide to help with your identification of rocks and minerals.
- Organize and display your rocks by characteristics such as grain size, color, mode of origin, etc.
- Organize and display your minerals by characteristics such as color, hardness, lustre, etc.

Make a Geological Map

- Obtain a large-scale topographic map of your area.
- Take field trips along the roads and railroads to examine as many rock-cuts as possible. Look for rock exposures along streams or on accessible hills and ridges.
- Watch for places in which different rock types are in direct contact.
- At each exposure, try to identify the rock type. Shade in its location on the map. Use a color-coded legend to group the rocks in the area.
- Looking at the exposures you have colored in, imagine how the rock types would join up. Trace in the assumed contacts between the different rock units.
- You have now made a geological map of the area! Try to determine the relative ages of the different rock units, the order in which the rocks were formed.

Grow your own crystals

- Place 2 or 3 charcoal briquettes (or lumps of coal) into a small shallow bowl and put the bowl in the center of a plate or aluminum pie pan.

- Thoroughly mix 1/4 cup liquid bluing, 1/4 cup table salt, 1 tbsp. household ammonia, and 1/4 cup water until the salt dissolves.
- Place a few drops of food coloring at different spots on the charcoal.
- Pour the mixed solution over the charcoal so that it is surrounded. Leave it undisturbed for several days.
- Discuss how the crystals develop from chemicals. (The charcoal soaks up the solution, and as the water evaporates, crystals grow from the chemicals left behind.) Relate this to the growth of crystals in rocks.

Make rock crystal candy

- Put 1/2 cup of water in a saucepan and bring it to a boil.
- Remove the water from the heat and immediately stir in 1 cup of sugar until it is dissolved and transparent (about 2 minutes).
- Add a drop of food coloring.
- Pour the solution into a tall jar.
- Tie a long piece of string (2-3 times the height of the jar) around a stick and lay the stick on the rim of the jar so the string dangles and coils inside the jar. Keep the dust out by placing a small piece of paper towel over the top.
- Let it sit undisturbed for 2-3 weeks. The dissolved sugar will collect onto the string in sugar crystals.

Check Out the Atmosphere

Keep weather records

- Set out gauged cans to measure precipitation.
- Chart or graph temperature and precipitation changes.
- Build weather vanes or wind socks to determine the wind direction.

Build a model parachute

- Cut out a 30 cm. square piece of tissue paper (or use the wrapping tissue which comes around fruits at the store, or silk or cotton cloth).
- Punch a hole in each corner.
- Reinforce the holes with glue-backed reinforcements if you're using tissue paper (for extra strength, place one on each side of the hole).

- Cut 4 strings all the same length (about 30 cm), and tie one string through each hole.

- Tie the loose ends of the string together around a cork (or other weight).

- Embellish the parachute by attaching a paper or clay person to the cork.

- Cut a small hole in the center of the parachute to help it open more quickly.

- Fold up your parachute and throw it as high as possible.

- Experiment using different sizes and materials and folds for your parachute.

- Discuss gravity and air pressure.

Launch hot air balloons

- For the top of the balloon, cut a square, 50 centimeters on each side, out of tissue paper. Cut a 1 centimeter square from each of its corners so that you can fold the edges to make flaps.

- For the sides of your balloon, cut four rectangular pieces of tissue paper, each 76 cm x 49 cm. Then cut off two triangular pieces 30 cm x 14 cm from one end of each side. Mark a 1 cm wide flap along four of the edges of each side (see diagram facing page).

- For the bottom of the balloon, cut two 20 cm squares from a file folder. Cut out their centers, leaving 1.5 cm frames. Put a thin layer of rubber cement on one side of each frame. When the cement has completely dried, touch the cemented surfaces together carefully so that they are exactly lined up. They will bond instantly. Punch a small hole in the center of each side of the frame. Cut two pieces of wire 22 cm long and push each wire through the center of a cotton ball, and then attach to the holes in the frame.

- Now glue the sides and top of your balloon together. Start by applying a thin coat of rubber cement to the surface of part of the glue flap on side #1 and touch it to the edge of side #2 while it's still wet. Following the same procedure, glue side #2 to #3, #3 to #4, and #2 to the top. Next, glue each side to the top and then glue the edge of side #1 to #4.

Step 1

Step 2

Step 3

Step 4

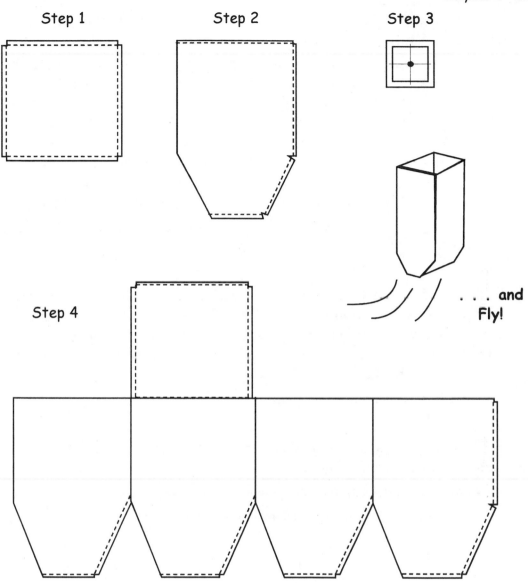

. . . **and
Fly!**

Glue the lower edges of the sides together and then glue the bottoms of the sides to the file folder frame.

☞ Launch your hot air balloon outside, in an open empty field. Gently open the balloon so it fills with air and hold it in upright position. Have an adult add a few drops of rubbing alcohol to the cotton and light it. Make sure the wind is coming from behind you as you launch the balloon, or do this on a windless day. As the alcohol burns, it will slowly fill the balloon with hot gases, causing the total mass of the balloon to decrease. The balloon will rise out of your hands because the cooler heavier air around the balloon will push it up. Let it go, and watch to see how high it will fly.

Explore the Forces of Nature

Friction

☞ Explore the benefits of friction as you encounter examples in your everyday lives – sand on icy sidewalks, different treads for different-purpose shoes, taped handles on hockey sticks, rubber grips on bicycle handles, "pocked" basketballs, snow tires. Visit a service garage and check out the brake system of a car.

☞ Explore ways to minimize friction:

   ☞ wax skis

   ☞ build pulley systems with Meccano or Lego, or set up a pulley system to help with everyday chores.

   ☞ experience how ball bearings minimize friction.

      ☞ Fill a bottle lid with marbles and cover it with a piece of cardboard.

      ☞ Flip it over and pull out the cardboard carefully.

      ☞ Carry objects around the floor on your lid.

Magnets

☞ Find examples of magnetic devices (toys, catches on cupboard doors, note holders, knife holders, telephone holders and pens . . .)

☞ Make your own games using magnets (fishing, travelling checkers, etc.)

☞ Use magnets to collect objects around the house.

- Experiment with the effects of one magnet upon another, like and unlike poles.
- Make your own magnet by stroking a nail with one end of a strong magnet.
- Experiment with the magnetic fields of different magnets:

  Place a magnet on a table and cover it with a piece of glass or paper.

  Scatter iron filings (or pieces of steel wool) on the glass or paper and tap it very gently.

Electricity

- Have fun creating electricity through friction (static electricity):

  Rub a balloon on your hair and then stick the balloon on a wall.

  After combing your hair briskly, hold the comb near a small stream of water from a faucet.

  Comb your hair briskly in a dark closet, listening for crackling sounds and watching for sparks. Relate this to the sounds and sparks of electrons jumping from one place to another in thunder and lightning.

- Appreciate the value of electricity in our everyday lives. Try an electricity-free day.
- Set up simple electrical circuits by connecting dry cells (batteries) to lamp or bell receptacles using switches and copper wire. Commercial electricity kits describe a number of activities and provide the needed equipment.
- Emphasize the aspect of safety while working with electricity. Discuss safety procedures in lightning storms or when encountering downed power lines.

Some Social Studies activities to have fun with while learning about the world:

Maps

Create a 2-dimensional globe

- Draw a world map on a grapefruit, using a permanent-ink marker.
- Peel the grapefruit carefully, keeping the skin intact.

- Make slashes so the grapefruit peel will lay flat.
- Compare the continent shapes on your map to those on a globe and on an atlas world map.

Make jigsaw maps

- Trace a map onto tracing paper, including any features you wish (mountains, rivers, cities, etc.)
- Cut out the tracing-paper map and completely glue it onto a larger sheet of poster board.
- Cut along the edge of the map, keeping the border in one piece.
- Glue the border onto another sheet of poster board to make the frame of the puzzle.
- Cut the map into puzzle pieces. Put all the puzzle pieces into a zip-lock bag and paper-clip it to the frame for storage.

Create contour maps to show land elevations

- Mix 3 parts salt and 1 part flour into water to make a heavy paste.
- Draw a map on a piece of heavy cardboard.
- Using the legend on an atlas map, build up different areas on your map to relate to different elevations.

History

Make a time-line showing the age of the earth

- Stretch out 3 centimeters of ribbon, representing 3000000 years, the length of time people have lived on earth.
- Add 62 more centimeters, representing the 65000000 years since the dinosaurs became extinct.
- Add 4500 more centimeters (45 meters) to this ribbon, representing about 4500000000 years, to indicate how long the earth itself has existed.

Create A Historical Time Line

- On a blank adding-machine roll, mark off the centuries, both B.C.E. (Before Common Era) and C.E. (Common Era) When learning about any aspect of history, document its date on the timeline. This enables your child to become oriented to historical dates and to see relationships.

Dramatize historical events to bring them to life.

Write "diaries" as your child learns about explorers.

Art Ideas and Recipes:

Art Techniques

Crayon Resist: Draw a picture, coloring in heavily with crayons or oil pastels. With broad brush strokes, cover the picture using a diluted water paint. This is especially effective for designing an undersea picture or a nightscape.

Rubbings: Lay a piece of paper over a texture. Using the side of a crayon or piece of chalk, make firm even strokes in the same direction, over the surface. Experiment with a variety of textures – brick walls, gratings, tree bark, screening, corrugated cardboard, coins, leaves, feathers, ferns, lumber, brass plaques, etc.

Simulated oil or acrylic paint: Mix rhoplex (liquid plastic) directly with powdered tempera. Add water if a thinner consistency is desired.

Fabric Paint: Add dry tempera powder to unbeaten egg white, making a paste. Add 1/2 tsp. of vinegar. Using this mixture, paint a picture or design on a washed and ironed fabric. Place the fabric face down between two sheets of plain paper, cover with a cloth dampened with vinegar and water, and press with a hot iron.

Reverse Painting: Place a small amount of bleach in a margarine tub. Dip the absorbent end of a Q-tip into the bleach and make a design or picture on a piece of tissue paper. Hang your picture to see the translucent effect. This is also a good method for creating African prints on brown construction paper.

Finger paint: Try a variety of recipes. A white vinyl table cloth and a garden hose provide easy clean up (or try it in the bathtub).

- Mix liquid starch (Glide) and tempera color until creamy.
- Mix wallpaper paste, cold water, and tempera color until creamy.
- Mix 1 cup white sugar, 1 cup flour, 5 cups cold water, and tempera powder. Boil until creamy.

☞ Chocolate pudding mix is fun to use, particularly with very young children or with children who are hesitant to "get dirty".

Art with Nature

A moss garden: Collect different mosses, wrapping each in damp newspaper to keep from drying until you are ready to create. Spread moss facing outwards around the inside of a large jar. Moisten the moss and keep the jar covered. Observe and try to duplicate the various shades of green using water paint and paper.

Leaf Spatter Prints: Place a sheet of paper on a covered table. Arrange leaves on the paper, vein sides down, and stick pins in to hold the leaves in position. Dip a toothbrush in watercolor paints, and rub the bristles on a wire screen held horizontally over the leaves. Let the paint dry and remove the leaves.

Iron-On Leaf Transparencies: Press leaves between newspapers for a couple of days. Place the flattened leaves on one side of a folded sheet of wax paper. Shred old crayons with a potato peeler, dropping the wax pieces among the leaves. Fold over the wax paper, and iron. Cut out the transparency in an attractive shape, punch a hole at the top, and display in front of a window.

Rock Art:

☞ Try carving a piece of soft rock with files and sandpaper.

☞ Wash a favorite stone, notice the patterns, and develop the patterns further with felt pens or enamel paints.

☞ Add buttons, sequins, wool, pieces of material, etc. to make a pet rock.

Petal Dye Painting: Go for a walk, taking along a bag to collect all kinds of different leaves and petals. When you get back, experiment by rubbing the different petals onto white paper, noticing the different natural dyes.

Spring Wind Catchers: Decorate a 50 x 20 cm. piece of heavy paper with felt pens, crayons, paint, wallpaper or paper scraps (use a theme motif, if you like). Attach streamers along one of the long sides. Roll the paper into a cylinder and staple. Punch 4 holes, evenly spaced, around the top edge. Insert yarn through these holes to form a hanger, and let it blow in the breeze.

Print Making

For printmaking ink, you can mix:

- 1 part liquid starch (Glide) with 1 part dry tempera to a heavy, tacky consistency, or...

- wallpaper paste, tempera color and water to a very thick paste-like consistency.

Gadget Prints: Experiment with a variety of objects, dipping them into a tray of "ink," then pressing them onto paper, making pictures and patterns. (Try spools, bottle caps, screws, bolts, potato masher, paper clips, feathers, feet, fingers, etc.)

Vegetable and Plant Prints: Brush "ink" directly onto a halved fruit or vegetable, or onto a leaf or fern. Press down onto a sheet of paper. (To make different shaped prints, cut raised sections in the halved vegetables.)

Plasticene Prints: Draw an image on a moist surface of clay or plasticene. Brush "ink" onto it, and print onto your paper.

Sponge Prints: Rub a damp sponge on a cake of tempera paint. Press onto a paper gently, overlapping different shapes and colors.

Cardboard Cut Prints: With an exacto knife, cut shapes from heavy cardboard. Arrange these shapes to make a design or picture and fasten them down to another piece of cardboard with glue. Roll "ink" over the raised surface with a brayer (or used paint roller). Place a paper on top of your inked cardboard and rub with the back of a spoon, lifting off carefully after testing a corner.

Styrofoam Prints: Gouge a piece of styrofoam (a meat tray works fine) with a nail or other sharp object, to make a design or picture. Pick up "ink" with a paint roller and roll onto the styrofoam. Lay a piece of paper down on the inked surface and rub with a spoon. Lift the paper off carefully.

Roll-a-Print: Cut a design or picture from light cardboard (or use string, rick-rack, etc.), gluing it on a cardboard tube or metal can. Roll the cylinder across the "ink." Then roll the cylinder across your paper to make borders.

Create Your Own Paper

1. Make a slurry by filling a food blender 2/3 full of water and adding 1 cup of 1/2-inch pieces of scrap paper slowly. Experiment by adding fibers,

such as grass clippings, dried leaves, rose petals, onion skins, etc. Blend thoroughly.

2. Make a strainer for your slurry by attaching a piece of fine screening to a wooden frame.

3. Strain the slurry, holding the screen over an empty dishpan and pouring slowly, to distribute the slurry evenly over the screen. Lay paper towel on top of the screen and squeeze out the water as evenly as possible, pressing from the center out.

4. Turn the screen over on a stack of newspapers. Lift the screen off carefully.

5. Iron the hand-made paper when it's almost dry, then peel off the paper towel.

6. Experiment with making colored paper by using colored pieces of scrap comics to make your slurry, or by adding fabric dyes, food coloring or tea.

Sculptures

String Sculptures

1. Saturate a piece of string in a thick flour and water paste, slipping it through your thumb and finger to remove any extra drip.

2. Form a figure or shape with the string on a piece of wax paper (more than one piece of string can be used as long as the end portions are secured with more paste). If you are making people, coil the string for a head, outline the limbs and finally fill in the torso with continuous lines.

3. Allow your string sculpture to dry thoroughly.

Sculpture blocks for carving

1. Gently sprinkle Plaster of Paris into an equal quantity of water, sifting through your fingers.

2. Stir carefully and slowly until it begins to thicken.

3. Quickly pour the mixture into a container, such as a milk carton.

4. Peel the container away when the block has set, and you are ready to carve. Keep it in plastic wrap between work sessions.

or:

1. Mix water with 3 parts of vermiculite and 1 part of plaster and set as above.

2. Mix water with 1 part sawdust and 1 part plaster and set.

3. Mix 2 parts sawdust, 1 part plaster, and 1/2 part of wallpaper paste and set.

Play Dough

There are many recipes, but this is one of the best.

1. Mix 1 cup flour, 1/2 cup salt, 1-2 tbsp cream of tartar in a medium pot.

2. Add 1 cup water, food coloring and 1 tbsp cooking oil.

3. Stir over medium heat, 3-5 minutes, until it forms a glob in the middle of the pot.

4. Cool and store in sealed containers. (Keeps a year!)

Salt Ceramic Ornaments

1. Stir 1 cup of salt, 1/2 cup cornstarch, 3/4 cup water and food coloring (optional) in a pan.

2. Cook the mixture over medium heat, stirring constantly until it's a thick blob.

3. Remove from heat, and place the mixture on a piece of foil.

4. When it's cooled a bit, knead thoroughly and form into ornaments.

Baker's Clay

1. Mix thoroughly 1 cup salt, 4 cups flour, 1 1/2 cups water and 1/2 cup of liquid tempera (optional), adding a bit more water if necessary.

2. Knead dough 5-10 minutes.

3. Allow items made with colored dough to air dry. For uncolored dough, bake at 300 degrees for 1 to 2 hours on foil-lined baking sheets. When cool, paint and then spray with clear varnish.

Nutty Play Dough

You can eat what you make!

1. Mix 1/2 cup smooth peanut butter, 1/2 cup honey, and 1 cup dry powdered milk.

2. Mold into shapes for eating. (If too wet, add more powder.)

Papier-Mache

Dry Method:

1. Tear newspaper into strips.

2. Crush a wad of newspaper into a ball, or create a base using boxes, bottles and cylinders of newspaper with masking tape. A balloon makes a great base for a papier-mache globe, a piñata or a piggy bank.

3. Cover your base with strips of paper, dipped into wallpaper paste (or a flour and water paste).

4. Overlap the strips, pressing down and smoothing out each time you add a strip. Add as many layers as you like.

5. Dry, paint and cover your sculpture with a glossy finish.

Pulp Method:

1. Tear pieces of newspaper and soak in water for 3 or 4 days.

2. Rub until the pulp shows no sign of print.

3. Squeeze out most of the moisture.

4. Mix the pulp with wallpaper paste (2 tbsp. to each cup of pulp).

5. Add salt and a few drops of oil of cloves (optional).

6. Press the pulp into different shapes, making puppet heads, trays, dishes, animals, etc.

Clay

- Use soft clay for beginners, storing it wrapped in plastic sheeting in a covered bucket.

- Before use, "wedge" the clay to make it more flexible, taking a melon size lump and pounding it into a slab. Fold over one side, then another, and pound again. Continue folding and pounding until the consistency is uniform.

- If the clay is hard, break up the big lumps and place them in a bucket. Poke holes in the clay and fill them with water. Cover the bucket and leave it overnight.

- If the clay is completely hardened, break it into small pieces with a hammer. Fill a bucket half full of clay pieces and cover with water. Set it aside for a few days, letting the pieces absorb water until they disintegrate. Mix the wet clay, let it settle, and then pour off excess water. Allow the clay to stand for a few days until the extra water evaporates.

Modeling tips:

1. Encourage the natural handling of clay to make shapes – pinching, pulling, patting, squeezing, smoothing, cutting, bending, twisting.

2. When joining, moisten both parts with your finger. Then roll your finger or a little round wooden stick over the joints with a rotating motion.

3. Don't let appendages stick out too far, and don't make them too thin.

Decorating tips:

1. Impressing designs – Using simple tools (sticks, spoons, nuts, bolts, screws, buttons, string, seashells, pine-cones, etc.), press into clay at regular intervals.

2. Incised designs – Scratch in the clay with a sharp tool (comb, nail, needle, etc.). Then, smooth the clay with a damp sponge and dry slowly.

3. Relief designs – Cut away the clay surrounding a design. Then, round all the sharp edges of the design by smoothing with a dampened finger-tip.

4. Inlaid designs – Remove sections of clay from different parts of the design (about 1/4 inch deep). Fill these depressions with clay of a different color. After the clay has dried, rub the surface with very fine sandpaper.

Geometric Shapes

- Plasticene and toothpicks: Form small balls of plasticene and join the balls together with toothpicks to build triangles, hexagons, cubes, etc.

- Newspaper cylinders: Create giant geometric shapes by rolling two sheets of newspaper together diagonally into long narrow cylinders. Cut off the weak ends and hold the cylinders together with masking tape.

Foil Masks

1. Cut a piece of cardboard into the shape of a face.

2. Draw lines on the cardboard to indicate features (eyes, eyebrows, nose, mouth, wrinkles, warts, etc.)

3. Glue string onto the feature lines.

4. Crush up tinfoil, open it up and spread it over the face, gluing and pressing to make a close connection around the string.

5. Paint the depressed parts black, leaving the string features silver.

Puppets

Sock Puppets

1. Pull an old sock over your hand so that the heel is over your thumb.

2. Add buttons, bows, yarn, fabric scraps, etc. to create your puppet.

Box Puppet Theater

1. Cut a large square window in the front of a box and a large portion out of its floor. Cut a hole near the top of each side for the curtain dowel.

2. Attach a curtain along the dowel, covering the front window.

3. Paint the inside of the box.

4. Balance the box between two chairs (or other uprights), sit under it and introduce your puppets through the box floor.

    or:

☛ If you have a large container box, cut a screen out of the top half, add a curtain and decorate. Stand or sit inside, under the screen.

"Stained Glass"

Candle Holders

1. Coat the outside of a small jar with a thin layer of white glue (slightly thinned).

2. Apply a small piece of tissue paper and re-coat the area with glue to make it shine and to keep the paper smooth.

3. Continue applying tissue paper and glue, sometimes overlapping, until the jar is covered.

4. Wind a piece of string around the neck of the jar and allow it to dry.

5. Trace each colored shape with a black felt-tipped pen to give a stained-glass effect.

6. Cut a candle so that it's about half the height of the jar and fix it upright by setting it into soft wax drippings.

7. Light the candle and enjoy the colors.

Windows

1. Draw an object or abstract design on a piece of cardboard. The lines must all meet and should be fairly simple.
2. Place Saran Wrap over the design, fastening it with masking tape onto the table.
3. Cut pieces of butcher cord the correct lengths, laying them over the lines of the drawing. (If it is to be hung, attach a loop of cord to the top of the design as well.)
4. Permeate the pieces of cord with white glue, full-strength, and glue them over the lines of the drawing. Let the framework completely dry.
5. Paint the design thickly and evenly using food coloring and white glue (can be diluted with water and stored in small covered jars - put plastic wrap between the bottle and lid to facilitate opening).
6. Carefully release the design from the Saran Wrap, and clean the outside edges with an exacto knife.
7. Place your "stained glass" in front of a window.

Noodle Beads

1. Place 1/4 cup of raw macaroni into each margarine container.
2. Stir 4 to 5 drops of food coloring into each container.
3. Pour the macaroni onto pie plates to dry.
4. Use these colored noodles for stringing into necklaces or bracelets, or for creating picture mosaics.

Chapter 8

How to simmer it all together . . .

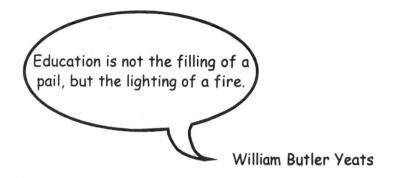

Education is not the filling of a pail, but the lighting of a fire.

William Butler Yeats

In fact, the fire is already lit. Children are born ready to learn, eager to explore and discover. Your task is simply to keep the fire burning – to comfort as the embers glow, providing love and acceptance, to fan the sparks with ideas and enthusiasm, and to add new experiences and skills as the flames take hold. A life-long learner is not a spectator waiting to be fulfilled, but an active participant in his own education, needing only support, encouragement and an environment rich in stimulation. Let him feel the satisfaction of discovery and the anticipation of what comes next. Let his imagination fly as he explores an idea. Follow it and jump on with both feet. Your child will establish the pace and backdrop theme while you incorporate timely and needed skills.

Themes may evolve from your child's interests:

As Amanda paints a rainbow, join in her awe, appreciating this wonder of nature, and grab her zest for learning as you, too, try out new ways to see the world. Encourage her to list what she already knows about rainbows and what she wants to learn, and then discover even more! The whole family can search for rainbows in any form as you visit the library, look over video rentals, check out paint samples at the hardware store, and skim magazines. Amanda could create her own rainbow by spraying a water hose into the sunshine, viewing the colors of the light spectrum through a prism and experiencing the thrill of making connections between them. Legends or stories of fantasy can be explored together and used as models for writing her own rainbow booklets. By providing a variety of art materials – tissue paper, paint washes, pastels, magazine mosaics, murals, natural dyes – she will be inspired to explore new ways to represent rainbows. She might enjoy composing poems or skipping chants or singing color songs. Along the way, you can integrate math activities developing skills at her level, whether it's matching numerals in a paint by number, skip counting by sevens while counting the arcs of rainbows or calculating ratios to blend the paint colors.

As you join in her adventure, the theme will open, allowing further investigation and divergent thinking. Emphasize creativity, taking each idea one step further – who knows where it will lead you! One child may try blending dyes to design a rainbow-colored T-shirt while another might explore arcs – those caused by the folding of mountains or the erosion of rock, or those of human-designed architecture. Opening a theme allows your child to pursue her unique interests, following her own styles of learning.

You may want to brainstorm for "first things to come to mind" when beginning a theme, jotting down thoughts and suggesting related new ideas. He will make the theme truly his as he goes off on his own tangents. Along with his ideas, you can integrate other activities which will further develop the skills your child needs or is having difficulty with. Before making his kite, Jeremy and his Dad tossed around ideas about kites, making a cluster map.

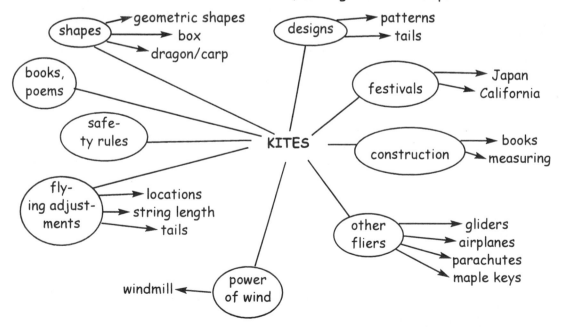

They gathered information and Jeremy eagerly began to design his kite following the instructions from a library book and experimenting with aerodynamics as he launched different kite types. After a quick lesson in multiplying mixed numbers, he increased each measurement by 1 1/2, making his kite larger than that described. He tested out options to determine the most airworthy qualities of kites. Later, Jeremy might diverge off into wind or airplanes, or even into the culture of Japan by constructing a Carp Kite for Children's Day. Absorbed with kites, Jeremy is gaining knowledge and practicing needed skills at the same time. His learning is relevant and meaningful.

Themes are dynamic, constantly changing and evolving. Ashley's interest in the water strider may evolve into a full-fledged pond study or a comparison of pond and meadow insects, or she may take a completely different twirl into figure skating, researching Elvis Stojko. Jimmy's study of the layered hillside may develop into a geologist's fascination with earth structures and rock formations. He may follow up on a fossil discovery, or learn more about glaciers, or even volcanoes and earthquakes. Justine's new puppy suggests a wealth of activities - from graphing the pets of the neighborhood, to calculating the cost of dog food over the year, comparing its tracks and prints to those of other animals and learning how to care for a sick pet. As Marianna observes the snowflakes on her jacket, an opportunity is presented for a study of symmetry, pattern and geometry; as it melts, her learning can move into world climates or even the science of molecules.

If a theme is being developed at school, help your child to make the subject his by pursuing a new angle. Leapfrogging on your enthusiasm for Mexican food, Brian's study of Latin America could take on new life with the intrigue of Mexican festivities. He might enjoy organizing a celebration party for the class, trying new recipes, making decorations and invitations, finding appropriate music, and researching appropriate activities. Focusing on his own interest within the school topic will make the study uniquely his.

A theme can be as short as a day (those Super-Saturdays!) or more than a year - your child's interests will move him along, possibly developing into a related topic or jumping to a whole new idea. Some days, the theme may simply evolve around the day's activities. Other ideas may simultaneously be developed along with a long-term theme. Be flexible. Remember that the theme is simply the inspiration around which learning connects. As long as your child is interested, she will learn!

Themes can involve the whole family in co-operative experiences. When an interest sparks and books are gathered and projects considered, the enthusiasm is often contagious. By opening up the theme, everyone can participate with his own ideas, at his individual level. After watching the rocket launch on television with her family, Sarah covered boxes with aluminum foil to make a space suit. Curious as to her needs for a trip, her older brother was soon busy gathering information about the planets and the conditions she would experience. Her sister eagerly began a papier-mache model of the solar system, exploring distances and related planet sizes. Her Mom researched types of dried foods and squeeze-containers to solve eating mishaps in space while her Dad was intrigued by stars beyond our system. Each person inspires the others but the complexity of the activities depends on individual interest and level of maturity.

The schoolhouses of the past benefited from multi-ability groups by having older children help the younger children. This is a good technique, allowing the older child to review and get his thoughts in order, reinforcing what he already knows and taking it to a deeper level . . . we never learn so well as when we have to teach others. Involvement in a single theme makes the idea of multi-ability groups even more valuable. Younger children present fresh and unusual perspectives, inspiring an exciting exchange of ideas and insights.

Themes may develop from a family business or from a hobby:

Businesses and hobbies are themes themselves, integrating skills and knowledge while pursuing a focused interest. Parents model work techniques and children absorb the social, physical and intellectual skills simply by being close. As your child takes on responsibilities in the business, he develops these skills further, using them to solve real problems. Caring for chickens on his family's farm, Kevin learns the correct amount and type of feed, the best ways to handle the hens and gather eggs, the technique of sorting eggs by size and quality, and the procedures of pricing and selling the eggs. Whether your family makes jewelry or furniture, designs inventions or web pages, farms or prospects for minerals, try to include your child at a meaningful level. Volunteer work (in hospitals, day care facilities, plant nurseries, etc.) develops responsible social behavior as well as introducing new interests and real-life skills. Pursuing a hobby or starting his own business - delivering newspapers, walking neighborhood dogs, cleaning yards, baking pies, making craft items for sale, shoveling snow or cutting grass

- will have valuable results, worth far more than any money made! These on-going "themes" provide occasions for real-life problem solving and develop patience and perseverance over a long period of time. Other themes and interests can evolve alongside.

Themes may develop from a family celebration or a holiday trip:

Whenever a celebration or holiday engages your child, the motivation for learning is high. Holidays mean special decorations, representative activities, specific foods, and lots of fun and excitement. Grandma's birthday can inspire curiosity about family history, a re-enactment of family traditions or a study of ancestral countries. Graphing the ages of family members or making booklets to tell about each member is fun and worthwhile. In preparation for the party, there's shopping lists and baking, card and gift-making, napkin folding, poems to write, pictures to draw and activities to plan. Even if your family doesn't celebrate a holiday, it can still be fun to put on a dragon dance or make lanterns for Chinese New Year. Invite friends and have a feast! Themes developed around holidays of the world provide exciting opportunities to learn about the people and traditions of other countries.

Family trips, as well, inspire themes. Anticipate your trip to the aquarium by gathering ocean books and magazines, making murals or booklets, and learning about the sea together. Your child will take that enthusiasm and knowledge with him to the aquarium, noticing details he never would have noticed otherwise. A skiing trip is an occasion to measure temperatures and snow depths, to observe animal tracks and homes, and to follow maps. Preparing for a trip to Mexico, browse through gift stores or art magazines to copy patterns as you create your own colorful piñatas and traditional clay pots. Try some of the foods you might encounter. As your child gathers and organizes information, your family will all become involved, checking to see what the weather may be like in order to pack suitable clothing and recreational equipment, making lists of places to see and activities to try. By acquiring geographical and historical background, he will recognize familiar aspects and be open to new experiences as he travels. Imagine visiting the pyramids with no information about their purpose or the way they were built. Yes, we would be in awe, but we can appreciate much more when we come with background. Your child, too, can gain much more from a trip if he is prepared for his experience. Just to drop off at Craigellachie on a quick trip through the Monashee Mountains will mean little. If, however, your child has previously dramatized hammering the last spike, he will see the site as the connection to join all of Canada. He will absorb history with his visit and be fully involved.

While celebrating holidays or travelling on short or long trips, you will be reading recipes, notices, and pamphlets together, writing plans or letters, and solving math problems as you encounter them. A daily journal (or special diary) will provide a record of the occasion.

Themes may develop from favorite books:

Books can be jumping off points, inspiring new interests and adventures. A science fiction novel might spark an interest in space travel or into a thorough study of the universe. A non-fiction book on birds might develop into an interest in bird calls or animal tracks. "Hans Brinker and the Silver Skates" might spur a need to know more about the dikes of Holland. After reading Pinocchio, your child might want to find other books in which lying is an issue or explore the topic on a sociological angle. Your child may get hooked on a "Franklin" theme - anxious to collect all the books, playing Franklin games, doing Franklin puzzles, dramatizing stories while manipulating Franklin characters, or verge off into a study of real turtles. "Little House on the Prairie" might lead to a theme on early pioneers, enacting and learning more about their hardships and lifestyle. Dioramas could be created to develop scenes for her own pioneer stories.

Whenever your child shows an interest in following up an author, a plot, a setting, a character or an issue, she is motivated for many new learning activities and experiences. Be alert to these opportunities, and have fun with them.

Themes can be purchased as unit studies:

Unit studies, coordinating all subject areas under a general theme, can be purchased at educational or teacher supply stores. They usually include activity suggestions for different levels and can be useful resources. It may help you to look through some of these, but ideally, you and your child will want to make up your own themes, following your child's unique interests, his own style of learning and his particular needs.

Themes integrate activities into whole learning experiences:

As we go about our everyday activities and pursue our own interests, we are constantly gathering information and acquiring skills. Our learning is not of individual subjects, and usually not a conscious effort, but rather an accumulation of experiences which impart skill, knowledge and inspiration. Only in looking back do we recognize all we have gained. This is a natural process where education is spontaneous and relevant, the result of experiences.

While Janine helps her mother wash the breakfast dishes, she is engaged in a social activity as well as accepting responsibility to her family. At the same time, she may be sharing ideas and thoughts, counting glasses, sorting silverware, reading labels, composing fun rhymes, dancing to her favorite music, a whole gamut of activities, completely spontaneous and unplanned. Her daily routine is providing many incidental learning experiences. Interests, hobbies, family holidays and books also provide opportunities around which learning can be integrated. By encouraging your child and being enthusiastic and involved yourself, you expand these opportunities into whole learning experiences.

Occasionally take a look back, however, checking to see that the skills your child needs are being included, and that the activities provide for all areas of his development - physical, mental, emotional and social. By incorporating all aspects of the brain, your child will see relationships and be better able to retain ideas and information. His thinking will be stretched as he has fun making connections. Notice which areas have been developed in your theme and which areas could be given more emphasis.

We have included an example circle wheel to help specify the accomplishments of your child, recognizing the brain realms of music, art, math, environment, physical activity and communication (to and from, written and verbal). A separate circle, mapping social and solitary activities, alerts you to a need for both interpersonal (with other people) relationships and intra-personal (within yourself) development. Our completed example of a unit on Space shows ideas of activities in each area. For some of your themes, create a large wall chart, as described at the end of this chapter, and engage your child in jotting down her activities in their appropriate areas. Remember that development of one area may be particularly strong with one theme, and only lightly touched upon in another theme. What may appear to be weak in the theme may have been developed strongly in other aspects of your child's day. Don't try to artificially

Our Space Theme

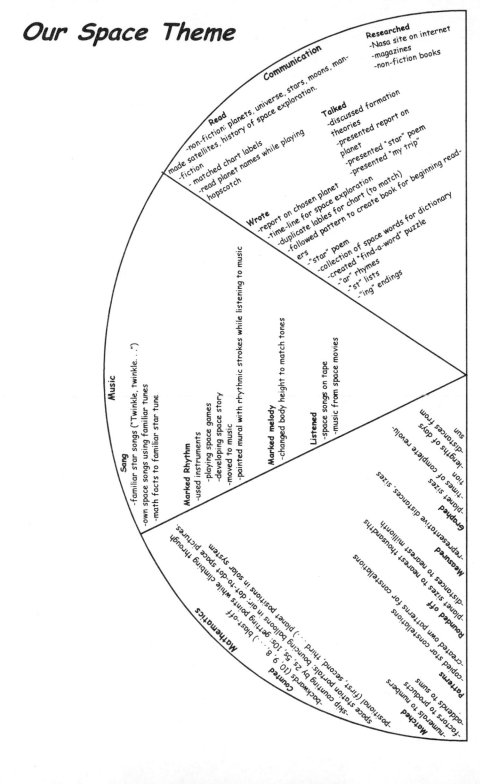

Communication

Researched
-Nasa site on internet
-magazines
-non-fiction books

Read
-non-fiction: planets, universe, stars, moons, man-
-fiction
- matched chart labels
-read planet names while playing hopscotch

made satellites, history of space exploration.

Talked
-discussed formation theories
-presented report on planet
-presented "star" poem
-presented "my trip"

Wrote
-report on chosen planet
-time-line for space exploration
-duplicate lables for chart (to match)
-followed pattern to create book for beginning readers
- "star" poem
-collection of space words for dictionary
-created "find-a-word" puzzle
- "ar" rhymes
- "st" lists
- "ing" endings

Music

Sang
-familiar star songs ("Twinkle, twinkle...")
-own space songs using familiar tunes
-math facts to familiar star tune

Marked Rhythm
-used instruments
-playing space games
-developing space story
-moved to music
-painted mural with rhythmic strokes while listening to music

Marked melody
-changed body height to match tones

Listened
-space songs on tape
-music from space movies

Mathematics

Counted
-backwards (10, 9, 8......) blast-off
-skip counting by 2's, 5's, 10's:
space station portals; bouncing balloons in air; dot-to-dot space pictures.
-positional (first, second, third...) planet positions in solar system.

Matched
-numerals to numbers
-factors to products
-addends to sums

Patterns
-copied star constellations
-created own patterns for constellations

Rounded off
-planet sizes to nearest thousandths

Measured
-distances to nearest thousandths
-representative distances, sizes

Graphed
-planet sizes
-times of complete revolution
-lengths of days
-distances from sun

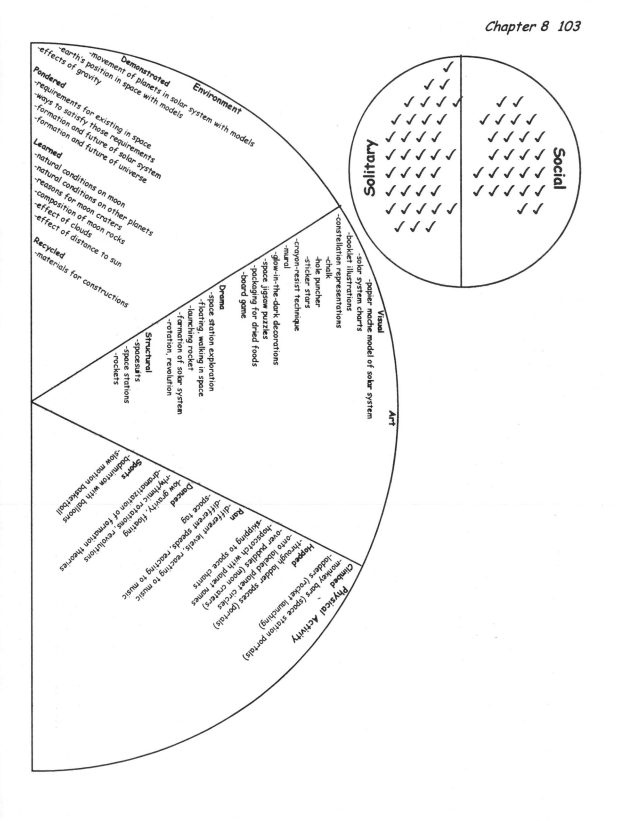

Environment

Demonstrated
-movement of planets in solar system with models
-earth's position in space with models
-effects of gravity

Pondered
-requirements for existing in space
-ways to satisfy those requirements
-formation and future of solar system
-formation and future of universe

Learned
-natural conditions on moon
-natural conditions on other planets
-reasons for moon craters
-composition of moon rocks
-effect of clouds
-effect of distance to sun

Recycled
-materials for constructions

Art

Visual
-papier mache model of solar system
-solar system charts
-constellation representations
-booklet illustrations
-chalk
-hole puncher
-sticker stars
-crayon-resist technique
-mural
-glow-in-the-dark decorations
-space jigsaw puzzles
-packaging for dried foods
-board game

Drama
-space station exploration
-floating, walking in space
-launching rocket
-formation of solar system
-rotation, revolution

Structural
-spacesuits
-space stations
-rockets

Physical Activity

Climbed
-monkey bars (rocket launching)
-ladders (rocket launching)

Hopped
-over puddles (moon craters)
-hopscotch to space charts
-onto labeled planet circles
-through ladder spaces (portals)

Ran
-different levels reacting to music
-different speeds, reacting to space chants
-space tag

Danced
-different speeds, reacting to music
-rhythmic rotations, revolutions
-low gravity, floating

Sports
-dramatization of formation theories
-badminton with balloons
-slow motion basketball

Solitary

Social

add things just to fill in the chart. If you notice that the physical level seems skimpy, just be sure your child is getting large motor activity in some other part of his day – a swim, a hike or some games at the playground. If the musical area is not being developed thoroughly, she might be interested in learning an instrument or joining a choir. If most activities are solitary, incorporate more activities in which he can work with others. If her day is predominantly social, try to establish more time for individual work and reflection. By occasionally following up on a chart like this, you ensure that your child is engaged in a well-balanced program, providing for her needs yet following her heart.

Enjoy the experience of learning with your child, developing themes and pursuing dreams together. Learning occurs when "fun" happens! With his imagination sparked, your child will enjoy life-long, self-directed learning as he ventures into endless possibilities. And it all begins around your kitchen table!

Create your own theme charts to track your child's progress

On a sheet of paper at least 21 inches wide and 17 inches tall, draw a large circle approximately 12 inches in diameter and a small circle approximately 6 inches in diameter. Create divisions within the circles and label them, as indicated below. Place the chart where both you and your child can see it.

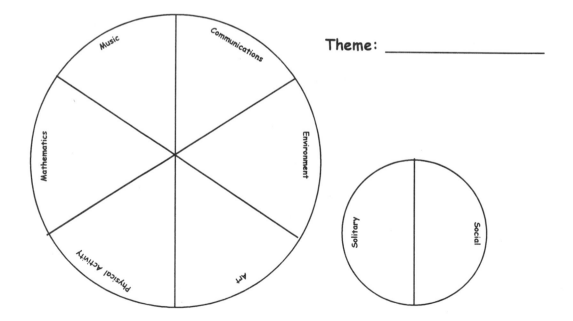

Chapter 9

How to get more information . . .

You're never alone. As you begin to enjoy "school" at home, you will discover many other families sharing educational experiences. Social activities may develop around similar interests. You may want to co-ordinate a cultural festival, a field trip or skating days with other families, or just meet to discuss themes, successes and concerns. Recognize that parents become involved at different levels and for different reasons. The schedule which works for one family may be entirely impossible for another family. The learning style of one child will be different from another's. Share your ideas and take the suggestions you can use, but don't feel intimidated or pressured to conform. Begin with your child's interests, at his pace, and together you will develop a unique program which works for your family.

Home Schooling Organizations will give you a start, putting you in touch with other home schoolers or groups in your area.

In Canada:

British Columbia

Canadian Home Educators
Association of B.C.
c/o 6980 Marble Hill
Chilliwack, B.C. V2P 6H3
President: Colleen Erzinger
Phone: (250) 493-0338
Fax: (604) 794-3940

Or

B.C. Homeschool Association
6225-C 136 Street
Surrey, B.C. V3X 1H3
Phone: (604) 572-7817
Fax: (604) 572-7832

Alberta

Alberta Home Education Association
President: Dan Ferguson
P.O. Box 3451
Leduc, Alberta T9E 6M2

Saskatchewan

Saskatchewan Home Based Educators
403-22nd Street West, Suite 13
Saskatoon, Saskatchewan S7M 5T3
Phone/Fax: (306) 545-3532
Toll free: 1-888-233-7423

Manitoba

Manitoba Association for Schooling at Home
c/o 185 Rossmere Crescent
Winnipeg, Manitoba R2K 0G1

Ontario

Ontario Federation of Teaching Parents
Herb Jones, Administration
145 Taylor Road West
RR 1
Gananoque, Ontario K7G 2V3
Phone: (613) 382-4947

Quebec

Quebec Association for Home-
Based Education
Veronica: 276-6984
Teresa: 424-4892
Marguerite: 284-2187
Jacquie: 484-3404 or
e-mail to jacqtrad@total.net
Liz: (819) 322-6495 or
e-mail to zil@intlaurentides.qc.ca

Or:

Quebec Home School Advisory
C/O Elizabeth Edwards
Box 1278, 1002 Rosemarie
Val David, Quebec J0T 2N0

Nova Scotia

Nova Scotia Home Education Association
C/O Marion Homer,
RR #1, Rose Bay, NS B0J 2X0
Phone: (902) 766-4355

New Brunswick

Home Educators of New Brunswick
Lawrence Mather
9 Garrison Drive
Renforth, NB E2H 2V1
Phone/Fax: (506) 847-4663

Newfoundland

Mr. and Mrs. Dean Stairs
96 Sullivan Avenue
Gander, NF A1V 1S2
Phone: (709) 256-7246

Prince Edward Island

Paul and Diane Luce
Box 3958 Central
Bedeque, PE C0B 1G0
Phone/Fax: (902) 887-3216

Northwest Territories

Inuvik Home Schooling Group
Box 2285
Inuvik, NWT X0E 0T0

Yukon Territory

Yukon Home Educator's Society
Box 4993,
Whitehorse, YT Y1A 4S2
Phone: (403) 663-2420

For **LEGAL** advice in Canada, contact:

Home School Legal Defence Association of Canada
203 - 1601 Dunmore Road S.E.
Medicine Hat, Alberta T1A 1Z8
Phone: (403) 528-2704/Fax: (403) 529-2694
They can provide you with a free summary of the education laws, relating to home schooling, in your province.

In the United States:

National Homeschool Association
P.O. Box 327
Webster, New York USA
145800-0327
http://www.n-h-a.org/

This address links to local home school associations in the US, resources, legal information, magazine subscriptions, etc.

Washington

Washington Homeschool Organization
6632 S. 191st Place, Suite E 100
Kent, Washington 98032-2117
Phone: (425) 251-0439

Idaho

Neysa Jensen
1809 N. 7th Street
Boise, Idaho 83702

Oregon

Oregon Home Educator's Network
P.O. Box 218
Beaverton, Oregon 97075-0218
Phone: (503) 521-5166

Montana

Montana Coalition of Home Educators
P.O. Box 43
Gallatin Gateway, Montana 59730
Phone: (406) 587-6163

California

Homeschool Association of California
P.O. Box 2442
Atascadero, California 93423
Phone: (850) 426-0726

Nevada

Homeschool Melting Pot
Nancy Barcus
1778 Antelope Valley Ave.
Henderson, Nevada 89012
Phone: (702) 269-9101

Utah

Utah Home Educators Association
P.O. Box 167
Roy, Utah 84067
Phone: (888) 887-UHEA

Arizona

Apache Junction Unschoolers
P.O. Box 2880
Apache Junction, Arizona 85217

NATHHAN (NATionally cHallenged Homeschooler Association Network)

5383 Alpine Road SE
Olalla, Washington 98359
Phone: (206) 857-4257
Fax. (206) 857-7764
http://www.geocities.com/Heartland/Ranch/6544/nathan.html

This association publishes newsletters and contacts with other families with similar needs.

GREAT SPOTS ON THE INTERNET:

If you have access to the internet (libraries often make access available free of charge) a good source for Canadian home schoolers is the **Canadian Home Based Learning Resource Page** at

http://www.flora.org/homeschool-ca/index.html

This site provides links to the provincial and territorial home schooling associations, a chat room, a mailing list, magazine subscription orders, home schooling conference information, curriculum resources, pen pals, and home schooling news. From the Provincial Association sites, you can then link to the distance-education pages, support groups, and legal information for your province.

A good U.S. reference is **Jon's Homeschool Resource Page** at

http://www.midnightbeach.com/hs/

Many LEARNING RESOURCES are available. I have included a few specific suppliers and curriculum resources. For further information, check the **Learning Resources Distributing Centre** at

> http://www.lrdc.edc.gov.ab.ca/

or the **Home School Internet Catalogue** at

> http://www.homeschool-nasco.com/

or **Homeschool Discount** at

> http://www.homeschooldiscount.com/

Gateway Learning Corporation – Hooked on Phonics, Hooked on Math

> 665 Third Street
> Suite 225, San Francisco
> California, USA 94107
> Phone: 1-800-ABCDEFG
> http://www.hookedonphonics.com/

The Learning House - especially helpful for Canadian History and Geography

> Harold and Louise House
> 8 Dunlop Drive, RR #4
> Goderich, Ontario N7A 3Y1
> Phone: (519) 524-5607

Home Training Tools - Science equipment

> 2827 Buffalo Horn Drive
> Laurel, MT 59044-8325
> Phone: (800) 860-6272

International Linguistics Corporation - Foreign language studies

> 3505 East Red Bridge Road
> Kansas City, MO 64137
> Phone: (800) 237-1830

ACE - Accelerated Christian Education – complete curriculum from Kindergarten to grade 12

> Rev. C. K. Fear
> Canadian Christian Academy
> P.O. Box 40
> Maidstone, Ontario N0R 1K0
> Phone: (519) 250-0061
> Fax: (888) 781-1114

Moore Canada - curriculum and resources from K to Grade 12

> 4684 Darin Court
> Kelowna, B.C. V1W 2BC
> Phone: (250) 764-4379
> Fax: (250) 764-0365

Math -U – See – a manipulative based K to Grade 10 math program

Western Canada:

Richard Knight
7 Sunlake Way
Calgary, Alberta T2X 3E3
Phone: (800) 255-6654
       (403) 254-9493

Eastern Canada:

Debbie Eckmier
310 Blucher Street
Kitchener, Ontario N2H 5V9
Phone: (519) 742-2482

Saxon Math

108 Windsong Drive
Stockbridge, Georgia 30281
Phone: In U.S. (800) 401-9931
Out of U.S. (770) 474-5341

Or:

For the Love of Learning
Caroline Penner
P.O. Box 68097,
162 Boonie Doon Mall
Edmonton, Alberta T6C 4N6
Phone: (403) 431-2861
Fax: (800) 429-6544

Box Cars and One-Eyed Jacks - ready to use manipulative Math games

> Joanne Currah, Jane Falling, Cheryl MacDonald
> 3930 - 78 Avenue
> Edmonton, Alberta T6B 2W4
> Phone: (403) 440-MATH
> Fax: (403) 440-1619

REFERENCES:

Magazines:

Quest: The Canadian Home Educator's Digest
Dick and Joanne Barendregt
12128-95A St. N.W.
Edmonton, Alberta T5G 1R9
Phone/fax: (403) 674-3002
http://www.telusplanet.net/public/plough/index.htm
- published quarterly, available on Internet

112 Kitchen Table Classroom

    - teaching tips, letters from Home schoolers, pen pal opportunities, publications, curriculum information, etc.

Practical Homeschooling
P.O. Box 1250
Fento, Montana 63026-1850
Phone: (314) 225-0743
- published quarterly

The Teaching Home
P.O. Box 469069
Escondido, California 92046-9069
Phone: (619) 738-2379
- published bimonthly

Books:

Atwell, Nancie (1987). *In the Middle – Writing, Reading and Learning with Adolescents.* Boynton/Cook Publishers.

Bosak, Susan V., Bosak, Douglas A., and Puppa, Brian A. (1991). *Science is . . .* Scholastic Canada Ltd.

Biggs, Edith, and McClean, Robert (1969). *Freedom to Learn.* Addison-Wesley.

Brown, Stephen, and Walter, M. (1983). *The Art of Problem Posing.* Lawrence Erlbaum Associates.

Forester, Anne D., and Reinhard, Margaret (1990). *The Learner's Way.* Peguis.

Goodman, Vera (1995). *Reading is More Than Phonics.* Reading Circles, Calgary, Alberta.

Kronick, Doreen (1993). *All Children are Exceptional.* Scholastic Canada Ltd.

Montessori, Maria (1948). *To Educate the Human Potential.* Kalakshetra.

Strongin, Herb (1985). *Science on a Shoestring.* Addison-Wesley.

Terzian, Alexandra M. (1994). *The Kids' Multicultural Art Book.* Williamson Publishing.

Wolsch, Robert A., and Wolsch, Lois A. (1982). *From Speaking to Writing to Reading.* Teachers College.

Whiten, David J., Mills, Heidi, and O'Keefe, Timothy (1990). *Living and Learning Mathematics.* Heinemann.